H³: Health, Healing, & Happiness

The Complete Guide to Holistic Healing

By

Christopher K. Sembera (BS, CNC, Be.P)

© 1995, 2002 by Chris Sembera (BS, CNC, Be.P). All rights reserved.

No part of this book may be reproduced, stored in a retrieval system, or transmitted by any means, electronic, mechanical, photocopying, recording, or otherwise, without written permission from the author.

ISBN: 1-4033-4407-8 (e-book)
ISBN: 1-4033-4408-6 (Paperback)

This book is printed on acid free paper.

1stBooks – rev. 11/15/02

DISCLAIMER

Please be advised that the information in this book is to be used as an educational guide and/or model for healthy living. It is not meant to serve as a prescription or treatment for anyone trying to heal themselves. The author also expressly disclaims any responsibility for any liability, loss, or risk, personal or otherwise, which is incurred as a consequence, directly or indirectly, of the use and application of any contents of this publication. Therefore, if you are sick, it is instead recommended that you consult with a medically trained physician.

ACKNOWLEDGMENTS

I would like to thank all of the people who assisted me in the publication of this book. This list begins with my parents for their love and unending support, which lasted throughout this entire process. Gratitude also goes out to Mrs. Elizabeth Houlder for her pre-editing help and Gregory D. Bunch for his numerous computer and editing services. In addition, I also must thank all of the numerous people who helped me along the way to finding the answers to my health problems. This is a long list which includes Dr. Zenia Richler of the Academy of Bio-Energetics, Dawne Torres of Biomeridian, Arthur Scott, DDS., Dr. Sherry Rogers and her staff, Dr. James Carter, and the nurses and staff at Complementary Medical Services, Dr. Yvens Laborde, and Chiropractor Marc Behar, Shirley Saylors-Clarkson and Mary Minto of Agape Center, and all of the staff at the American Chiropractic Clinic.

But, I especially want to thank God for all of the blessings that I have received in this life.

FOREWORD

The challenge to a person trying to regain their health is to obtain accurate information in an easily understandable format. It needs to be a reference book as well as a story of regaining health. You have both in *Health, Healing and Happiness.*

When I read *Health, Healing and Happiness*, I was thrilled that Chris had the stamina to go from one modality that had ceased to work for him, to another modality with such a positive attitude. Chris knew something was out there that would give him his health back. Chris first and foremost has faith and hope.

Chris does not offer a magic bullet approach to a cure. He offers a whole body concept of wellness. He states that if you do not care for your whole body you will not be able to recover your health.

As Chris takes you on his journey to wellness he shows you his backward steps as well as his forward motion. This mix allows you to feel the anguish he felt over his failing health, however, he also allows you to feel the joy as he found the modalities to put health and his life back together.

In *Health, Healing and Happiness* he gives us insights into nutrition, emotional health, education, stress reduction, reduction chemical exposure, heredity, exercise as well as other information.

He offers in this book the highlights of his research experience. He takes you through the steps of how to implement a wellness plan and how to achieve a balance in your lifestyle.

During Chris' experience he has searched for a balance in health care. He has close working relationships with both the medical profession and the holistic modalities. He has been on a quest to join the two to achieve his wellness and he has accumulated a wealth of knowledge in his travels to find a way to heal himself. He presents it to you in *Health, Healing and Happiness.*

Chris gives you back your hope and lets you know there is an answer out there. So don't give up, keep looking.

I invite you to enjoy your journey through *Health, Healing and Happiness.*

Dr. Zenia Richler
Academy of Bio-Energetics

INTRODUCTION

Welcome! In purchasing this book, you have taken the first step toward a healthier, happier way of life. Simply because, it shows that you are willing to take an active role in your health and well-being. This is important because the human body can only function optimally when all of its needs are fulfilled.

Health, Healing & Happiness is intended to serve as an educational reference and guide, helping people make wiser lifestyle choices. It is based upon my nine years of research and personal experience and contains what I believe to be the best information on holistic living.

Although there are no guarantees in this world, the strategies in this program hold the potential to enhance every single aspect of your life. This is because, developing your own personal health plan is one the most beneficial things that you can do for yourself. It helped me develop a clear focus on the truly important things in my life and how the way that I was living my life would never get me where I wanted to be.

You will also learn the elements of holistic living that I have concluded to be the most effective for restoring and maintaining wellness. These elements include discussions on the importance of: nutrition, prioritizing, love, spirituality, positive attitude, environment, exercise, heredity, maximizing digestion, and taking action. It is essential that a proper balance of all ten of the above mentioned factors be accomplished. In so doing, the individual is then prepared to maximize the quality of his life.

It is also necessary to understand that all success in life is founded on five basic principles, **(1) understanding where you are, (2) knowing where you want to go, (3) knowing how to get there, (4) believing that you can fulfill a goal and (5) your desire to achieve it**. These five principles feed all of the other ingredients, which are indispensable for rejuvenating and preserving wholeness. My entire program therefore attempts to nourish and expand these five key qualities.

For when we understand and utilize these five principles, we will be in a position to experience **Health, Healing, and Happiness.**

TABLE OF CONTENTS

Disclaimer iii
Acknowledgments v
Introduction vii
Chapter 1: My Story 1

Chapter 2: Health Building Qualities 30
    A) Open-Mind
    B) Form a Partnership With Your Physician
    C) Take More Responsibility for Your Life & Health.
    D) Self-Analysis Without Judgment.
    E) Find a Purpose For Your Crisis.
    F) Your Right To Make Mistakes.
    G) Perseverance.
    H) Long-Term Perspective.
    I) Listen To Your Body.
    J) Support Groups.
    K) Knowledge.

Chapter 3: Self - Destructive Qualities 39
    A) Prejudices.
    B) Rationalization.
    C) Holding Onto Past Emotions.
    D) Procrastination.
    E) Fear Of Failure.
    F) Blaming Others For Your Situation.
    G) Wanting Something For Nothing.
    H) Addictions.
    I) Self-Pity.

Chapter 4: Everything Counts 44

Chapter 5: Prioritizing 46
    A) Prioritizing Values.
    B) Value Exercises.

Chapter 6: Spiritual-Growth 49
    A) The Spiritual World
    B) Spiritual Regression
    C) Love and Forgiveness
    D) Miracles.
    E) The Tools of Spiritual Enhancement.
        1. Prayer.
        2. Meditation.
        3. Listening to God (Our Conscience)
        4. Attending Church Servives.
        5. Spiritual Education.

Chapter 7: Love.. 59
    A) A Loving Relationship with God.
    B) Self-love.
    C) Love of Your Significant Others.
    D) Willing Provide Loving Service to Others.

Chapter 8: Positive Attitude.. 65
    A) Expect Good Things To Occur.
    B) Reframing.
    C) Embrace Obstacles.
    D) Visualization.
    E) Positive Affirmations.
    F) Associate With Optimistic, Supportive People.

Chapter 9: Optimum Eating.. 72
    A) The Relevance of Nutrition.
        1) C.I.A. Factor.
    B) Denatured Foods.
    C) Essential Fatty Acids.
    D) The Health Reducers.
    E) Diet & Supplements.
    F) Vitamins, Minerals, and Other Supplements.
    G) Nutritious Eating.
    H) Optimum Foods.

Chapter 10: Maximizing Digestion 118
    A) Proper Mastication.
    B) Eating In an Orderly Manner.
    C) Eat More Foods That Contain Digestive Enzymes.
    D) Abstain from Eating 3 Hours Before Bedtime.

Chapter 11: Environment 121
    A) Supportive People.
    B) Education.
    C) Reduction of Unnecessary Chemical Exposure.
    D) Stress Reduction.
        1) Meditation/Reflection.
        2) Time Management.
        3) Enjoyable Career.
    E) A Happy Home.

Chapter 12: Exercise 130

Chapter 13: Heredity 134
    A) Prevention Continues to be an Unpopular Approach.
    B) Scientific Studies tend to support the beliefs of society.
    C) The greatest boundaries which humans possess are those that are self-inflicted.
    D) Inherited genetic patterns remain until your death.

Chapter 14: Taking Action... 139
    A) Hope.
    B) Faith.
    C) Courage.
    D) Goal Setting.

Chapter 15: Helpful Hints 151
    A) Health, Food, and Dietary Tips.
    B) The Five Taste Sensations.
    C) Organizational Tips.
    D) Lifestyle Suggestions.
    E) Question and Answer.

Chapter 16: Recipes, Juices, And Menus 169
    A) Juicing.
    B) Cooking Tips.
        1) Whole grains.
        2) Beans.
    C) Recipes.
    D) One week menu.

CHAPTER 1
MY STORY

You can if you think you can...Norman Vincent Peale

Over the course of my life, my health and well-being has covered a vast range, from the deep, dark lows of chronic illness, to the high level of health which I currently enjoy. To provide you with a complete understanding of my journey, it is necessary that I share my entire health history with you. Covered is both the regression and restoration of my health, plus all relevant factors leading up to that point. In this way, you will be able to clearly see all of my initial warning signs and where lifestyle improvements and wiser choices could have addressed many of my difficulties at much earlier levels of imbalance.

My story begins immediately after my birth, when all indications were that I was a very healthy and happy baby. Since my mother decided not to breast feed me, I was given a formula while at the hospital. This formula appeared to agree with me quite well as I slept very soundly and was a great joy to be around. (Or so my mother says.) Two days later, I was released from the hospital and my mother placed me on a cow's milk formula. At first, I seemed alright but each day I was a little less happy. I also began to have diarrhea and cried much more frequently. By my tenth day, these symptoms grew more pronounced, and I became very irritable and began violently spitting up my formula shortly after feeding. My mother was obviously very concerned and notified my physician of these symptoms. He suggested that I be fed barley cereal, hoping that it would help alleviate my problems. Unfortunately though, the result of this attempt was that blood began to appear in my stools. (Recalling this incident for my mother was very easy because it occurred the weekend of President Kennedy's assassination.) After the gastrointestinal bleeding surfaced, my mother stopped the barley cereal and called the physician. He then recommended that I switch to a soy-based formula, which my mother did. The gastrointestinal bleeding stopped shortly afterward, and over the next three weeks the severity of my symptoms became far less intense. None of these symptoms totally went away especially the diarrhea, which occurred quite frequently. However, at least the bleeding had ceased and I was able to keep my symptoms at lower levels of intensity.

Then at six weeks of age, a skin rash and bronchial mucous discharge developed. To help with this problem my physician prescribed the anti-histamine drug diametane. Although this alleviated my newfound symptoms, everytime that the diametane was removed from my daily regimen, the rash and bronchitis would return. Thus, my physicians had me continue the diametane until I was five years old. From that time on, it was used on an as needed basis.

Around my 10th birthday, my sinus symptoms had become progressively worse. My physician determined that an allergist was needed to test me for sensitivities. So off I went to see an allergist. He performed a number of tests and found that I was suffering with many allergies, which required addressing. Allergy extracts were prepared and provided a great deal of relief, particularly for my sinuses. Although it was necessary for me to stay on these shots until my junior year in high school, it was a big help to my situation.

Then around the time of my 12th birthday came a huge event in my life. My dentist found that I had an abscessed nerve in my front upper right tooth and required a root canal if we were to save the tooth. Since it was a front tooth, my dentist chose not to do the root canal surgery and instead recommended an endodontist who was supposedly very skilled at performing this procedure. We chose to follow this advice and allowed the endodontist to perform the root canal. All appeared to go well at first, yet little did I know that this would become one of the biggest mistakes of my life.

At the age of 13, a dermatologist was sought for relieving my newly present facial acne. He treated my symptoms with an ultraviolet light and a broad range antibiotic, which I took for over two years. About a year and a half into the antibiotic treatment, severe abdominal pain surfaced. (I am convinced that this was when the second wave of my gastrointestinal difficulties began.) To counteract this problem, I was sent to a gastrointerologist who simply placed me on the stomach relaxant, donatol, and told me to stop worrying. Even if I had been worrying, which I was not, a more complete and logical approach would also have included providing me with the name of several good books on stress management, along with some healthy dietary and lifestyle recommendations. In contrast, I was only medicated in order to relieve the intestinal pain, without any suggestion of lifestyle adjustments which could have provided more long-term relief to my ailing abdomen. The donatol did successfully alleviate most of the pain, but I was now beginning to experience inordinate amounts of gas and bloating. Nonetheless, I learned to live with this discomfort and moved on.

The next several years went by without any major problems and I even considered myself to be a rather healthy individual, who just had excessive gas, some additional allergies, and skin problems. I tried to rationalize this by stating, after all everyone has some difficulties. Right? Interestingly we often hear people say things like, "I'm healthy except, I lack energy, or I have arthritis." Upon further analysis, I later learned that these statements are simply not true. Instead, we must understand that unpleasant symptoms are typically only present when a problem exists. What's more, if we fail to rectify an ailing situation, then it could develop into an even bigger problem.

It was around 1980-81 when my root canal tooth began to turn brown. In spite of its less than optimal appearance, the tooth did not cause me any pain so I really wasn't very concerned about it. In fact, I even convinced myself that it did not look that bad. Instead, I was more concerned with all of the fun that is associated with the junior and senior years of high school.

My next warning signal came in 1983, when at the age of 19, I was diagnosed with mononucleosis. This setback appeared to quickly pass and within a couple months, I was back to my normal schedule. However, each winter afterward, a penicillin shot was needed to counteract my newly developed yearly bout with strep throat. Alarm bells should have been going off in my head that my state of health was deteriorating. Yet, I never even suspected that my health was descending and could be headed for greater difficulties.

The next episode came a few years later in October of 1986, when I began to experience severe joint pains, starting with my left knee and elbow but later spreading to virtually all of my joints. Upon seeing an orthopedic specialist, the anti-inflammatory drugs Dolobid and Ibuprofin were given from which only temporary pain relief was noticed. The Ibuprofen provided the most benefit, so when the prescription ran out I purchased the non-prescription strength, Advil. Through experimentation, I found that when I took five pills, four times a day for a total of twenty, that I was getting more relief than I did from the prescription version. This initially allowed me to continue on with my daily activities. However, it was not long before this too was unable to bolster me to the point where I was able to live with the pain and continue exercising. Thus, I was eventually forced to stop working out at the gym and jogging which were great hobbies of mine. My inability to keep exercising had three key negative consequences. First, it took away much of my strength, vitality, and endurance to which I had grown accustomed. Second, it removed a powerful stress reducing activity from my life which was very helpful to me. This was a huge loss as it was a great tool for blowing off steam, particularly if I was burdened with something. But maybe most important was the fact that missing workouts caused me to very rapidly lose about ten pounds, most of which seemed to be lean muscle mass. This had a very devasting effect on my overall self-confidence as I had taken great pride in maintaining a high level of physical fitness. After an entire year had passed with no real progress, it became apparent that some other strategy was going to be necessary. However, the doctors that I was seeing only had more of the same ineffective drug treatments to offer.

Around this time, my mother ran across an article in a magazine about the benefits of acupuncture and thought that it might be a viable option for me to pursue. With nowhere else to turn for help I decided to give this healing method a try. The first couple of visits brought very little difference. However, after the third or fourth treatments my elbows and knees began to show moderate improvement. Then about a month into these treatments, my joints although stiff and sore regained most of their range of motion. By the time I had completed two months of therapy, I was able to reduce the arthritic pain enough to resume exercising. Even though it was necessary to apply ice to my joints before and after each workout, I was nonetheless ecstatic to be able to revive my exercise regimen. My conditioning improved over time as did my confidence level, however, my joints still continued to ache.

The next episode came in May of 1989, when without warning, I was hit with a very intense pain in my back, pelvic region, and the heel of my left foot. I scheduled an appointment with a physician that my father had previously seen. He ordered several tests and to his surprise found a bladder infection. In spite of this discovery, he could find nothing else that would be indicative of the type of back pain that I was experiencing. So he sent me to see an orthopedic physician to have some x-rays taken. Although he could find no problem with my spine that would cause the back pain I was having, he did make a passing comment that would come back to haunt me. He thought that a prostate infection could be causing much of my back pain. However, the other doctor who treated me for the bladder infection did not agree, so I did not think much of it then. Instead, to address my situation an anti-inflammatory and a pain killing drug were prescribed for my back pain and an antibiotic was given for my bladder infection. While both doctors agreed that my back pain would eventually go away, they had no idea about the source or future situation of my heel. This mess occurred at a time that should have been very joyous for me, having just earned a B.S. Degree along with landing the claims executive job I coveted with AMICA, a prestigious insurance company based in the northeast.

Over the next couple of weeks, my concern grew that I would be unable to attend AMICA's claim training program due to my poor health. The first two weeks of this episode, were excruciatingly painful leaving me virtually bedridden. Although, the intensity of the pain subsided a bit over the next few weeks I still felt awful. Nonetheless, I really wanted to go and decided that I had improved enough to attend AMICA's six-week training program in Providence, Rhode Island. Completing all the required coursework in the training program was difficult in my sickened state but I managed to get through it. Upon completing the training program, I was assigned to work at their Syracuse, New York, branch office.

During my 2 and a 1/2 year stay in Syracuse, my condition only continued to worsen. Throughout this time, I was treated by several more physicians, which again were only masking my symptoms by prescribing more and more medications. The result of using these medicines was to induce the development of two or three new unpleasant symptoms. I cannot be harsh enough to describe the scope and intensity with which these symptoms permeated every aspect of my life. By the start of 1991, these indications had now grown dramatically to include the following: chronic prostatitis, powerful headaches, fatigue, major brain fog, inability to concentrate, a shoulder that would occasionally pop out of socket (this hurt like hell), numerous food intolerances, very foul smelling stools, dramatic mood swings, unrelenting back, neck, hip, pelvic, lower abdominal pain, yellowing of the skin, a pain that radiated down both legs, periodic kidney pain, oral thrush, painful urethritis, poor circulation, and severe chemical sensitivities.

Probably the most painful of the above manifestations was my urethritis which felt as though it had a large chopstick-shaped object rammed inside my urethra. In desperate attempts to reduce this pain, I resorted to placing an ice cube directly to the underside of my urethra (penis). While this measure was uncomfortable, it did temporarily numb the pain. This type of bizarre approach became necessary because of the pure agony which I was experiencing. Other areas causing me pain were my lower back, pelvis, neck, rectum, and abdomen. Even sitting was an excruciating event, because my colon, which leads into the anus, was so horribly inflamed, and would produce a sharp like pain every time that I would sit down. Sleeping too became extremely difficult, as I would awaken several times a night due to severe back, neck, and pelvic pain. Thus the only escape I got from this suffering was the few hours of sleep that I would get each night.

One of the doctors who found something of significance was Dr. Kendrick, a urologist, who diagnosed me with chronic prostitatis. A bell went off in my head when he cited prostatitis as my diagnosis. I immediately recalled the physician back home in New Orleans who stated that the pain in my lower back could be caused by a prostate infection. To address the problem he of course prescribed more antibiotics and stated that they would temporarily kill the infection and my immune system, if strong, should be able to keep it under control. Well I tried this and once again it did virtually nothing to help. When I told him this, he decided to do a urethrascope so that he could internally view what was going on in my prostate. An appointment was scheduled and I had the examination done about a week later. When he examined my urethra and prostate, he found inflammation in the prostate area. He said that it was very red and inflamed but that it was something that I might have to learn to live with. When I stated that I was in constant, unrelenting pain, he said well there is nothing that could be done to rectify this matter so I might as well get used to it. At this point, I began to question what could be the underlying cause of the prostatitis, but all Dr. Kendrick could say was that the causes of prostatitis were unknown. As I was told this I naively asked, what if we just remove the prostate gland, would this help my situation? He responded by saying that now Chris if we do that you would likely lose the ability to have erections. But you know I was in such incredible pain that I even briefly, very briefly, considered discussing this further with Dr. Kendrick. That's how much agony I was in.

Another physician in Syracuse who I saw later treated me for oral thrush, arthritis, and prostatitis also told me that there was nothing more that he could do for me. To say the least, it became obvious that the physicians I was seeing had far too many limitations and it was going to take a more diverse base of knowledge to assist my situation. Because of this, I knew that I would have to keep looking until I could find a physician that had a somewhat different approach. Although I had no idea of where to look for such a doctor, I just passionately believed that one existed.

Then at last, on 2/21/91, came the first step for which I had been waiting. It occurred at a bookstore when my supervisor and I were looking for an anatomy book and stumbled upon a health book titled, *The Yeast Syndrome*, by Dr. J. Parks Trowbridge. My supervisor, Frank Carnevale, noticed the book and mentioned it to me noting that it may be worthy of my interest as he was aware of my situation. Prior to picking up the book, I thought that it would probably have little to offer me. However, immediately after skimming the pages, I saw many of own symptoms being mentioned and discussed. I quickly determined that Dr. Trowbridge's work was worthy of closer examination and purchased the book.

The Yeast Syndrome is a self-help health book which discusses the connection that exists between yeast infections and many chronic health problems. Dr. Trowbridge says that while candida overgrowths are typically synonymous with vaginal and urinary tract infections, they are also frequently associated with gastrointestinal disturbances. He further asserts that most cases of candidasis result from extended bouts with either broad spectrum antibiotics, steroids, birth control pills, or excessive consumption of sugary, refined foods. It should be noted that candida albicans (yeast microorganisms) are present in all humans. Yeast problems only occur when the balance between candida and the beneficial microorganisms are disturbed. An ideal ratio of microorganisms is assumed to be approximately 85% beneficial to 15% non-beneficial.

Due to the fact that digestive disorders are common in my mother's family, this approach made a great deal of sense to me. Plus, it seemed that the information in this book was really striving to help address an underlying cause to certain types of health problems. Those who have had to endure various digestive disturbances include my brother and mother, her father and especially my uncle Romeil. Poor uncle Romeil who lived to the ripe age of 83, suffered with severe regional Ileitis (Crohn's disease) for over four decades. (Crohn's disease is a chronic inflammation disorder that affects the lower part of the small intestine; in some cases the colon and other parts of the digestive tract are also affected.)

In spite of my family history, after reading Dr. Trowbridge's work, I felt confident that my situation could be improved. So I committed myself to trying practically anything which made sense in order to enhance my health. This effort started with the sugar-free, yeast-free, low-carbohydrate diet, which was in *The Yeast Syndrome*. Amazingly, within 2 days of starting the diet, I felt significantly better than I had in the past couple of years. While all of my symptoms were still very much present, there was a clear and significant reduction in their intensity. The key reason for this progress was that I had removed most of the main offenders like sugar, alcohol, caffeine, vinegar, white flour, white rice and other refined foods from my diet. Therefore, the candida was not being fed the key yeast promoting foods on which it could easily thrive. Probably the most impressive sign was that the joint pain which I had suffered with for the past 5 years was about 50 percent better. In spite of my improvement, within the next several weeks it became clear that although this program helped my situation, further assistance would be needed. Another good thing about *The Yeast*

Syndrome was that it provided the name of a nutritionally-oriented physician and author who practiced in Syracuse; her name was Sherry Rogers.

So I scheduled an appointment with Dr. Rogers, who is a highly regarded physician known as one of the true pioneers in environmental medicine. She had written a small section in *The Yeast Syndrome* and it seemed as though she would be a good fit for my situation. Upon meeting her it was obvious that she practiced the healthy lifestyle which she preached. She radiated health and had great confidence that as long as I studied her books and followed a health building program fit for my body's particular needs, I would get better. The tests that Dr. Rogers ran successfully detected a number of problems including an overgrowth of candida, numerous nutritional deficiencies, and various chemical and environmental allergies. In response, a healing plan was arranged which she calculated would help to resolve my unbalanced condition.

This approach included allergy shots, vitamin, mineral, and other nutritional supplements, exercise, environmental controls, and of course a health-building eating plan. While there was some modest initial improvement, my health situation quickly stagnated and it became obvious that this too would not bring the type of results that I was hoping to achieve. In response to my requests about what more could be done, Dr. Rogers suggested that I might consider trying a Macrobiotic diet. Macrobiotics is a health promoting lifestyle which centers around a vegetarian diet that focuses heavily on vegetables and whole grain cereals. Although, I was not a vegetarian I was desperate enough to give it a solid chance. So I threw myself into reading and learning more about the Macrobiotic diet and way of life. I found the information to be quite interesting and it helped me to learn more about how one would go about stimulating the healing process. (An interesting note that I learned during my exploration into macrobiotics was that the heels of our feet is on the energy meridian dealing with our bladder and urinary system. Thus, the pain that I was having in the heel of my foot was actually a signal that my prostate and bladder were ailing. This was of course confirmed by the bladder infection and chronic prostatitis which had earlier caused me great discomfort.) Although the Macrobiotic approach appeared to be helpful at first, after a few months of progress my healing came to sudden halt. Soon thereafter, my condition began to worsen and I started to lose weight. At first, when I began to lose weight Dr. Rogers said that it was to be expected, so I just thought that this was part of the process that my body would have to go through. However, over the next couple of months, I continued to lose even more weight. Many of my friends and co-workers were telling me how thin I was and how bad I looked but I disregarded their comments as I thought the weight loss was to be expected. However, I started becoming very weak and some of the most severe symptoms began to return. Then one day I decided to get on a scale which I had been avoiding to see just how much weight I had lost. To my shock, I had lost almost 40 pounds and was now down to just 108 pounds. I also went into my bedroom to see myself in a full length mirror, which I was previously staying away from because it bothered me to see myself so thin. Well to say the least it was a shock. It was like looking at someone who had been at a concentration camp; you could literally see all of my bones. At that moment, it was crystal clear just how sick I was and I knew that there was no way I could continue working and living so far from home. So shortly after this episode, I notified my supervisor that I would be resigning and returning to New Orleans. Although this was a huge step backward in my personal life, it was necessary due to my quickly deteriorating health. Still, I remained optimistic and thought that after returning home I would quickly get well.

After arriving home, I continued to stick with the Macrobiotic diet for about six more months. For the longest time, I just thought that I was doing something wrong and that I must work even harder to effectively rejuvenate my health. However, as I continued to deteriorate, it became very obvious that my situation was becoming quite severe and potentially life-threatening. At that point, I thought that Macrobiotics was a cure-all and if it did not help then I was probably doomed. Yet, my mother and father pleaded with me to see a local physician and call Dr. Rogers for a phone consultation. Because I could tell that they were so upset, I agreed to do both. First, I scheduled an appointment with a local gastroenteroligist, who saw me just a few days later. He did a very brief exam by feeling my stomach and lower abdomen and said that he could find no major inflammation. Therefore, in his opinion, it was unnecessary to proceed any further. To say the least this was the most pathetic excuse of an exam that I have ever experienced. I did not request that he look further because I knew from past experience that he would not like having his judgment challenged and would respond with some sort of smart ass response. After returning home from the appointment, I decided to call Dr. Rogers office to schedule a phone consultation. When I spoke with her, she was surprised to hear how badly I was doing. In response, Dr. Rogers suggested that I immediately try the opposite approach and eat a diet high in animal protein as this was likely what my body needed to repair itself. To say the least, I was surprised to hear this because of all the information that she had written about Macrobiotics and how effective it was in healing so many health conditions. My state of mind at the time, was that if a diet is healing for one then it must be healing for everybody. I just did not yet understand that there is no one single program that fits the needs of everyone. Instead, we all have our own special needs and so every program must be individualized to fit those needs.

So after speaking with Dr. Rogers, I decided to retry the high animal protein eating plan, which was actually quite similar to the candida or yeast-free approach which I had previously followed. It consisted mostly of meat, eggs, fish, low to medium starch, vegetables and strict avoidance of grains as they were serving as irritants to my gastrointestinal tract. In addition, she wanted me to add back more high quality sources of fat and sea salt to help repair my emaciated and weakened body. Plus, I now also found it beneficial and even necessary to chew my food at least 50 times per mouth full or else eating would cause too much gas to build up in my gastrointestinal tract.

This dietary approach provided great symptomatic relief, and I was able to slowly gain about 2/3 of my weight back over the next ten months. However, I still had a very long way to go if I was going to fully recover or even be able to live a semi-normal quality of life. Likewise, any deviation I made from these foods would quickly produce the return of my innumerable symptoms. In fact, it was so bad that eating one small serving of grains like brown rice or bread and my gut would start to spasm, severe abdominal pain occurred, and my stools become bloody. Then it would take about a month of strict dietary adherance to get back to where I was before eating the offending food. Thus, it was not very hard for me to comply with my limited eating plan. At this point, it became apparent that I was suffering with a very severe case of irritable bowel syndrome along with some gastrointestinal bleeding and ulceration.

Just as the eating plan needed to be revised to more accurately address my condition, so did my supplement formula which went through countless alterations. One reason that these changes were necessary was because my yeast related symptoms would flare up when taking supplemental iron which was present in my mineral supplement formulas. This move was actually counterproductive and helped to keep these pathogens alive and well in spite of all that I was doing. Likewise, many of the supplements which were labeled as hypo-allergenic also turned out to be irritating to my gastrointestinal system. Finding supplements which I thought were both effective and tolerable to my system took a great deal of time and research, but was an essential part of my journey.

As my efforts became more involved with this endeavor, it became clearly evident that I needed to take an even greater role in rebuilding my health and fully devote myself to healing. So to prepare myself for this endeavor, I set out to gain as much knowledge as I could about nutrition and natural healing. To do this, I enrolled and completed correspondence holistic nutrition programs through the American Holistic College of Nutrition, read and researched numerous nutritional books and magazines, and even took some cooking classes. This took a great deal of time and effort but it was something that I actually began to enjoy as I found it to be very interesting.

Additionally, I studied a number a different health building and healing diets. While none of these approaches fully addressed my needs, each contained key elements which proved beneficial. As long as I adhered to my restrictive dietary regimen, my symptoms would stay relatively in check. However, each time I would try to challenge myself by adding new foods, back would come the spastic colon, bloody stools, and so on. Well to say the least living like this was very difficult. I was unable to eat out because restaurants add so many extra or hidden ingredients which I could not tolerate. In addition, my stamina and energy levels were significantly reduced, severely restricting my ability to work. This period of time covered from 1992-1996, during which Dr. Rogers had me take a number of blood, stool and urine tests and was able to find even more nutritional deficiencies, a leaky gut, and gastrointestinal dysbiosis. Unfortunately the supplements that she was recommending were not agreeing with my system. So this left me hanging without knowing what to do to make my gastrointestinal tract improve sufficiently. I also saw a few physicians in New Orleans, but once again none of them could find anything of major consequence that could be causing my health difficulties. (It is my understanding that the reason they could not find anything was due to the particular tests they were running which would only have found a problem on the cellular level. At that point, most of my health problems had not quite advanced to that stage of degeneration. Instead, my problems were probably still mostly on an energetic or electrical level.)

In the early part of 1996, Dr. Rogers convinced me to retake an *Intestinal Permeability Test*. Its purpose is to help determine the condition and status of the gastrointestinal lining. When the results came in, it again showed that I was suffering with a leaky gut. A leaky or hypermeable gut as described in Dr. Rogers book, *Wellness Against All Odds*, is an inflammation of the gut lining which allows the passage of large food particles that normally are not able to pass into the bloodstream from the gut. Then as these larger than normal food particles enter the bloodstream our defense system begins to attack our own tissues. I am of the opinion that this scenario often then contributes to the development of a number of problems like arthritis, food allergies, fibromalgia, or even auto-immune diseases like Lupus or Crohn's disease. She had found the leaky gut problem two years earlier but again I was unable to tolerate many of the supplements that she suggested. I just kept thinking that I needed to find supplements which did not irritate my gastrointestinal tract, so I spent countless hours researching the ingredients in order to find the best tolerated supplements. While this helped me to find a couple supplements which were causing me problems, it was far from perfect as I would later have confirmed. One interesting note about leaky gut is that Dr. Rogers cites its main cause as the use of NSAIDS or non-steroidal anti-inflammatory drugs. As you earlier read, I had used these drugs extensively several years beforehand in response to the joint pain I was experiencing. This obviously placed a great deal of stress on my gastrointestinal system, which was already showing signs of imbalance.

After the results from the leaky gut test were received, Dr. Rogers also reordered another *Comprehensive Digestive Stool Analysis* to help determine the overall health of my gastrointestinal tract. The CDSA report showed two major reasons for concern. First, it detected that blood was present in my stools. This of course can indicate a number of things, the worst of which is probably colon cancer. It also found extremely high levels of a harmful bacteria, (non-lactose forming *e coli*), which suggested a profound alteration in bacterial gut ecology. Looking back, this condition was obviously exacerbated everytime I overused prescribed antibiotics. (This was especially true when I took antibiotics over a two-year period to help curb acne, my yearly usage of penicillin to fight strep throat, as well as the use of the broad spectrum antibiotic, Doxycycline, for recurring bladder and prostate infections.) The CDSA report also recommended that since blood was present in my stools, a sigmoidoscopy be used to determine its origin. So I looked for a gastrointerologist who had a nutritional background, and chose Luis Balart, M.D., one of the four authors of *Sugarbusters*. Dr. Balart performed the procedure but was only able to find evidence of a previous hemorrhoid. While I was somewhat relieved with the results, I was also quite frustrated as I still did not know how to resolve my situation.

Several months later, and with no clear-cut progress, my primary care physician and all around good guy, Yvens Laborde, M.D., wanted to get a good view of my entire colon and recommended that I have a *colonoscopy*. Part of me wanted to just eat foods which I knew would flare my gastrointestinal problems; this way I could know once and for all my exact diagnosis. However, I also knew that straying from my diet would flare up my worst symptoms which would be very painful and take some time for my gastrointestinal tract to return to my current level. So I decided to just stay on my restrictive eating regimen. Test was performed on March 5, 1998, by a gastrointerologist named Dr. Smith. He was successful in finding minor inflammation in the colon and evidence of previous hemorrhoids, yet nothing more was found. After getting these results, I told the physician of my restrictive diet and how I had wished that this test would have found something more definitive which could easily be remedied. However, he encouraged me to continue as I was doing and said that as long as I was able to keep my condition under control without the need for medication, that I was probably best off doing so. Although part of me was pleased to get these results, as well as Dr. Smith's encouragement, I was also frustrated that we were still unable to find a clear-cut cause to my digestive problems.

In desperation toward the end of 1998, Dr. Rogers and I again decided to try antibiotics in a frustrated effort to try and kill the bacterial infection in my gut. However, this proved to be a huge mistake as my symptoms only got more severe. I now had managed to develop even more food intolerances, to the point that even the natural sugars found in vegetables like carrots, beets, and winter squash would flare up my symptoms. Admittedly, even I was beginning to lose hope that I would ever get well.

The next couple of years were very tough, as I felt awful much of the time. I did get some initial relief as I experimented with a few products that helped me to moderate my symptoms like bovine colostrum, oil of oregano, Arctic Alginate (pharmauceutical grade sea algae), and olive leaf extract. Eventually though, even these products became less beneficial as my health continued to turn for the worse. This was most apparently noted by the emerging dermatitis rash on my right hand, the arthritis in my left knee, as well as the constant itching which I was experiencing. After going to a local dermatologist she prescribed a cortisone cream, which helped to bring the rash under control, however, my left knee was still flaring up and bothering me more than ever. Plus and even more important the lower back and kidney pain which I had experienced off and on for the past ten years was becoming more pronounced. The kidney pain concerned me most as some people with autoimmune diseases like Lupus frequently experience kidney disease. Then as the disease progresses, it can sometimes lead to the need for dialysis or even proceed to renal failure. To say the least this was a great concern for me. Once again, I was forced to stop exercising. In all honesty, I truly began to doubt whether or not there was anything that could be done to address my health situation. I knew that these pessimistic thoughts were detrimental but I was just so frustrated.

After conferring with Dr. Rogers, she thought that I needed to restart my mold and pollen allergy extracts to help address my dermatitis, plus test for heavy metals to see if I had elevated levels of mercury. She had earlier encouraged me to take the heavy metals test, but I just did not want to spend more money for seemingless endless expensive tests as I thought that I was already doing everything possible to rectify my situation. However, my situation had become very severe and so I was willing to give this additional test a shot. In terms of the dermatitis, she was correct. Almost immediately, the extracts helped to bring this skin condition under control but it did very little to help my left knee and kidney pain.

A few weeks after starting my new extracts I had a consultation with Dr. Rogers to discuss the results of the heavy metals test. The report showed that my mercury levels were more than five times the levels of what are considered to be safe. Over the years, I had seven cavities filled with mercury amalgams but I never really thought much about it or the possibility that they could become a problem. To say the least I was shocked and concerned not to mention worried about how we would effectively approach this situation. Dr. Rogers recommended a nutritional detoxification protocol to help remove the excess mercury from my system, but once again my gastrointestinal tract was unable to tolerate some of the supplements that she recommended, especially the all important glutathione and its precursors. (Glutathione is an amino acid which helps the body to detoxify heavy metals and other poisons.) The one saving grace was that adding the mold, dust and pollen extracts to my yeast and candida extracts, enabled me to resume juicing which provided great energy and highly absorbable nutrients back into my body. These juices provided great relief by helping to increase my energy levels so that I could make it through the day. Plus, I decided to try an anti-inflammatory and anti-parasitic nutritional product called MSM (Melthyl-Sulfonyl-Methane) or organic sulfur. It has worked for many people with heavy metal toxicity and inflammatory disorders, particularly those with arthritis. Fortunately it also helped me tremendously and my knee pain soon disappeared after using MSM.

The kidney pain though continued to persist leaving me with no apparent solution to address this situation.

While perusing the internet for help in dealing with mercury toxicity, I found an internet support group for those with mercury toxicity called, cfsn.com. This site is run by a gentleman named Jeff Clark who previously suffered with mercury toxicity but has since recovered. The great thing about this site is that people from sea to shining sea are able to e-mail various questions into the e-metals list while all participating members can read and respond to the various questions. Members not only include lay people but also dentists, doctors, and other health care professionals who were very helpful in quickly answering many of my questions which would otherwise have been very difficult to obtain. Although the information that is acquired in such a setting is typically more general and is not case specific, I still learned a great deal from the e-mail discussions.

Then on March 21, 2001, a life altering day for me, my chiropractor, Marc Behar called wanting me to come to his office and see a fascinating machine that could evaluate one's acupuncture meridians to find imbalances and stresses in the body. I was skeptical at first but Dr. Behar said that he had seen a similar system before and was very impressed with its accuracy and believed it to be a tremendous tool for evaluating health disturbances in the body. So I decided to go and see for myself. When I arrived I met Biomeridian regional sales representative, Dawne Torres, who was performing meridian stress testing on a few of Dr. Behar's patients. The one thing about Ms. Torres that immediately stuck out in my mind was her very fit physical appearance and the healthy glow of her skin. She truly looked the part of someone who was selling a health related testing device. Dawne informed us that what we were seeing was a form of testing known as electrodermal screening or EAV (electro acupuncture according to Voll) originated by German physician, Reinhold Voll in the 1950's. (Biomeridan's current version of EAV is called the MSA-21 or Meridian Systems Analysis.) When I asked Ms. Torres how her MSA machine worked, she stated that it works by measuring electrical resistance and polarization at acupuncture points and meridians. (It does this through the use of two cables which come from the MSA machine, one positive and one negative. The positive lead is attached to a stylus with an electrode

Christopher K. Sembera (BS, CNC, Be.P)

tip. The practitioner then applies the tip to one of the client's acupuncture points. At the same time, the client is holding the other cable, which is the negative lead, in their free hand. This process actually enables the client to form a complete circuit, and allows energy and information to flow from the MSA-21 to the probe, through the patient to the hand electrode and back to the MSA machine. The reading that is derived from this process is a measurement of how much electricity makes it through the circuit.)

During her visit, Dawne devoted ten minutes to testing each of us but during this time she evaluated a few supplements for me including an oil of oregano supplement which I was taking for the chronic yeast problems I was having. Contrary to what I thought about this product, she found that this supplement was not balancing my system. Upon seeing this I thought that nothing would be able to balance my meridians as long as my mercury levels are so high. However, she was very confident that we could find supplements that I would tolerate; her certainty made me want to learn more about this system. The day after the meeting, I sent an e-mail to Ms. Torres requesting that she schedule another appointment so that I could have a greater opportunity to see more of her and her MSA-21 machine. She responded with an e-mail and invited me to the Downtown Hilton where she would be attending an acupuncture seminar throughout the weekend. As you may have guessed, I jumped at the chance and went early Friday morning which was perfect because most of the people at the seminar were at a presentation. So to my good fortune, she was able to devote about 90 precious minutes to me. Per my request, she tested almost all of the meridians on my hands and feet, plus all of my supplements, and several of my teeth. During these evaluations, Dawne found several areas in my body which were under severe stress including my pancreas/stomach, colon/lung, and kidney/bladder meridians. In addition, she tested my old root canal tooth and several other teeth that contained dental fillings and found each of these teeth and their corresponding meridians to be unbalanced.

While most of my supplements were fine there were a couple including my digestive enzymes, and as earlier stated an oil of oregano supplement, which the MSA found to be problematic for my system. She then quickly proceeded to find several appropriate replacements that the machine showed would balance my acupuncture meridians.

Well over the next couple of months, I took the supplements which performed well during the testing session with the MSA-21 and felt noticeably better. At this point, I was reflecting on how much time and money I had spent over the years on various supplements which were supposedly hypo-allergenic but in reality were irritating to my gastrointestinal tract. If only I had known sooner about this extremely accurate evaluating tool, just think how much quicker I would have gotten well. Likewise, I thought to myself if only Dr. Rogers had an MSA machine, she could have quickly determined what approach would have been the best for me. Nonetheless, I still considered myself extremely fortunate to become exposed to this testing device at this time. In fact, five weeks after our session at the seminar, Dawne returned to our office and retested me on several of the meridians that had earlier been evaluated as being under great stress. As expected, this evaluation registered improvement in all of my weakened meridians but also showed that I still had a ways to go if I were going to fully recover. I was pleased to see and feel progress but I also knew that it was going to take an even greater commitment on my part.

Throughout this time, I was reading and researching on the internet and found a wealth of information about how dental work can affect the acupuncture meridians which run to our teeth. Probably the best illustration of this can be found at holistic dentist.com. It provides a map of the entire dental layout, which is shown below for your review.

According to acupuncture experts, our teeth are lined directly on certain energy meridians and when something is not biocompatible with these meridians the natural energy flow becomes disrupted and imbalances in the corresponding organs can take place. When I first saw this chart I flipped. My root canal was on the right upper front tooth which is on the kidney/bladder meridian which corresponds with my kidney weakness and previous bladder infection and prostatitis. Plus all of my teeth that had dental amalgams where

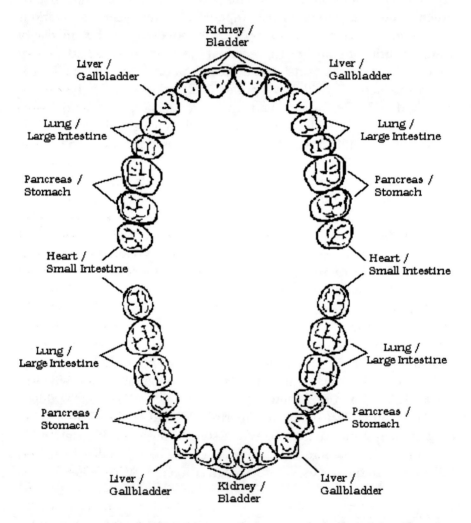

either on the large intestine or pancreas meridian which were the exact areas that Ms.Torres found major stresses in my body on her MSA-21 machine. Any lingering doubts that I had about the MSA were totally wiped away because I could clearly see the tremendous accuracy it had in evaluating the underlying imbalances in my body. Amazing, I thought after all the years of going to doctors who were supposedly experts in their field, yet none of them were nearly as accurate as the MSA machine.

At this time, I decided to find a dentist who could safely perform the dental work necessary to more thoroughly address my situation. After conferring with my fellow metalheads on cfsn.com, one of the members gave me the name of a biological dentist in Metairie, Louisiana, named Arthur Scott. Dr. Scott is known for using certain precautions to safely remove mercury amalgams and perform dental work with biocompatible materials. I scheduled an appointment with Dr. Scott for a cleaning and discussed how we would go about addressing my situation. After taking X-rays, he could find no apparent problem with my root canal. In spite of this, I was adamant that we take steps to effectively deal with my root canal as I had read that they typically house anaerobic bacterial infections. Dr. Scott then suggested redoing the root canal and filling it with the highly biocompatible material Biocalex, as he initially thought that this would be sufficient to resolve my situation. I also stated that I likely wanted him to remove my mercury amalgams but thought it was best to address my root canal situation first. Dr. Scott recommended that before we proceed further, I take a biocompatibility test to determine which dental materials would be best suited for my system. I concurred and had the test shortly after our appointment.

While waiting for the results of the biocompatibility test, I did a great deal more reading and research on root canals. During my studies, I learned that it is virtually impossible to sterilize the dentine tubules of teeth, which is a suitable site for microscopic anaerobic bacteria to reside. These bacteria produce a very toxic gangrene like debris which is so small that it can pass through the tubules to our mouth and into our blood stream. As a result, a continual strain is placed on the detoxifying organs especially our kidneys to eliminate these poisons. Unfortunately, we cannot kill these bacteria, as our white blood cells are too large to enter the dentine tubules. Dr. Weston Price, a dental researcher for the American Dental Association (ADA) in the early 1920's, completed a tremendous amount of research and documentation in this area. He found that many people who had root canals were frequently ending up with chronic and degenerative health problems. In fact, one man in his studies who had a root canal also was suffering with kidney disease but after having the root canal removed his kidney problem gradually healed. He then went one step further and surgically implanted the tooth into a rabbit. Amazingly within two days, the rabbit died of the exact same kidney ailment that the human host was experiencing. Sadly, much of this documentation has been ignored and is even viewed by the current ADA as inaccurate information. For those wanting to learn more about the potential problems which can occur with root canals read Dentist George Meining's, book, *The Root Canal Cover-up EXPOSED*.

After I told Dr. Scott that I wanted to have the tooth removed he recommended that I go to see Harold Kennedy, DDS an oral surgeon, to extract tooth, periodontal ligament and scrape the jawbone to remove any remaining debris. Failure to complete all three steps could lead to a cavitation, which is necrotic or dead matter developing in the jawbone. This could obviously cause numerous problems so it is absolutely necessary that these steps be followed. So I scheduled to have the extraction performed on June 5, 2001, by Dr. Kennedy and later in the day report to Dr. Scott's office to have a temporary bridge installed.

The day before extraction I met with James Carter, M.D., a physician who uses chelation therapy, nutritional IV's, as well as nutritional guidance to help address health problems like heavy metal poisoning. Due to my severe malabsorption of nutrients, I asked if I could obtain some type of nutritional IV which contained the amino acid glutathione. The reason I asked for this was because it so important in the detoxification of heavy metals and I had been unable to take it due to its acidic nature not reacting well to my leaky gut. He agreed with my assessment and prescribed what he called a Myers cocktail plus glutathione to be taken every time dental work was done or as needed but no more than once a week. This IV preparation contained: 100 cc of fluid, 50 cc of Vitamin C, 1 cc of Vitamin B-6, 1 cc of Vitamin B-12, 5 cc of magnesium chloride, 3 cc of calcium gluconate, 1 cc Vitamin B-complex, and 2 cc of glutathione. He provided me with a list of supplements that he recommended I take two weeks prior to removal of amalgams. I was already taking many of the same nutrients but using different brands which were evaluated on the MSA machine as compatibile with my system. Thus, I chose to stay with the brands that I was using. We then agreed to meet after amalgam removal to do a challenge test and then determine the next step for detoxifying the mercury from my system.

Well finally the day that I had waited for was now here. I was excited but did not really expect to get much better until at least a month after extraction. However, immediately after the tooth was removed Dr. Kennedy noticed a little gutta percha (the root canal filling material) lodged in my jawbone. He had to scrape the jaw for about five minutes to get it out but he eventually removed it all. Well amazingly within a half-hour after this procedure the kidney pain that had been bothering me for the past decade was dramatically improved. Hell yes! At last I was now starting to address the underlying causes of my problem. What Dr. Kennedy did for me was to remove a constant irritant (the gutta percha) from my jawbone which was located along the kidney/bladder meridian. In addition, he removed the tooth which was the source of a chronic bacterial infection which I was previously unable to address. It was also likely that this root canal was the underlying source and cause of my urethritis, as well as the prostate and bladder infections I experienced some ten years earlier. Plus, it also appeared to be an indirect contributor to my gastrointestinal problems as this tooth was continually flooding my body with toxic residue which it was unable to effectively eliminate.

If you want to know just how much I improved from this procedure, within two weeks, I was able to resume working in a full-time job, something I had been unable to do for the past nine years. In fact, my new job as a therapist at a chiropractic office required me to stand on my feet all day long, yet this posed no problem for me. One of the main symptoms that I still had to battle was that I remained highly chemically sensitive although not quite as bad as before. Plus, all of my food allergies persisted and my gastrointestinal tract remained irritated and sensitive to acidic things requiring me to continue following my very restrictive diet. At the same time, my gastrointestinal tract now began to really purge and cleanse itself of all the old fecal matter which it was previously unable to unload. As this stuff came out it made me really tired and even more sensitive to chemicals. However, once I would finish a wave of cleansing my sensitivities would be lessened and my gastrointestinal tract started to become more calm and relaxed. In addition, the dark circles under my eyes also began to slowly receed.

Well the next several weeks went by and I continued to make gradual but steady improvement. I continued using the Myers IV cocktails weekly for the next several weeks. In addition, I did weekly high temperature saunas to raise my temperature and thus aid in killing the bacteria and harmful microorganisms in my gut as well as helping to expel the mercury and other toxins from my system. Many people are unable to use hot saunas as they are sensitive to the heat, fortunately for me though I had no such problem. (For these folks far infrared saunas is likely the best approach.) I really credit this step to Earthrise Chlorella a chlorophyll-rich, sea algae which helped to loosen and cleanse the old, dried fecal matter from my gastrointestinal system. This is an important step as the gastrointestinal tract is where many of the harmful microorganisms find a place to reside. If this matter is removed then these parasites, bacteria, and viruses find it much more difficult to survive. Furthermore, if one is vigilant in providing a clean gastrointestinal tract then these deleterious microorganisms largely die off and are excreted by the body until just a small amount can survive. Then we are able to replenish our bodies with beneficial bacteria which keep the non-beneficial bacteria in check. Fortunately for me all of the hard work that I did throughout this process was really helpful in preventing my health situation from deteriorating to ultra serious consequences.

In addition, the other key thing required to continue my progression was to make certain that my main organs and systems of detoxification were functioning properly. These organs include my gastrointestinal tract, liver, kidneys, and my skin through sweating, as well as, my circulatory and lymphatic systems. Dawne would periodically come back to town and check the corresponding meridians for me to make certain that I was progressing properly. This is especially important for those who chose to have their amalgams removed, as many people that I have spoken with on the metals internet site who did not effectively nourish, cleanse, and drain their bodies before amalgam removal, got worse. One person that I used to correspond with even claims to have developed Multiple Sclerosis. The reason that this occurs is because when amalgams are removed one is exposed to a good dose of mercury. Thus, if the individual is not able to effectively detoxify this mercury, it will remain in the body and have further opportunities to do damage. Although good biological dentists use oxygen, rubber dams, double suction, air purifiers, and other precautions to help reduce the amount of exposure that one will have to endure, one will still be exposed to an increased level of mercury during removal.

It is my understanding that although mercury fillings can potentially cause problems for virtually everyone, typically a second factor arises which acts as a catalyst to make the host overly reactive to the mercury fillings. These other factors would likely include: emotional trauma, stress, chronic infections, presence of other heavy metals like lead or cadmium, or the overuse of medications. Chronic infections are very stressful to the body making it work overtime in an attempt to purify itself. Then the mercury, which naturally leaks from the fillings, creates another burden for the body to handle. If your body is not able to detoxify the mercury then it starts to store it, potentially leading to all sorts of problems. Another common cause is the use of more than one metal in dental work. This could include metal inserts, typically titanium, which are frequently used in the body to provide structural strength and then a second metal namely, mercury, is used in the formation of the amalgams. Apparently a battery type of effect is created in the body occurs that causes the mercury to wear down faster and be absorbed into the body where it can do so much damage. Both of these must be avoided if one is striving to achieve and maintain high levels of health and wellness.

My progress continued over the next several weeks. It was so wonderful knowing that I was heading in the right direction and having the confidence that everything I was doing was aiding my progression. Admittedly though, I was a bit concerned about the potential problems that could possibly arise when my permanent bridge was installed. Although the biocompatibility test claimed that the bridge materials which would be used were acceptable, I still had so many times been disappointed throughout my struggle that I had become a little less optimistic than I was prior to my illness. Nonetheless, August 14th, the day that permanent bridge would be installed had finally come. All went well on that day and over the next several weeks. It soon became obvious that the bridge was just fine and was a good fit for my system. Nonetheless, my progress seemed to be leveling off. I then decided to schedule to have my seven mercury amalgams removed as this was going to be necessary to progress and get to where I strove to be healthwise. I scheduled my removal and replacement to be completed into two different sessions. With the first session being set for September 4th and the second appointment scheduled for the 26th of September. In the intial visit, Dr. Scott removed and replaced three fillings. Throughout this visit Dr. Scott was wonderful. He and his assistants were very effective in supplying my body with the necessary oxygen and keeping the exposure of mercury to a minimum. In fact, the only clear noticeable side effects were mild headaches and brain fog, which continued a few days after initial amalgam removal session.

The next couple weeks went by without much of a hitch, while I waited for the 26th to arrive. I was so excited and pleased with the way things went during the first removal that I called Dr. Scott's office to let them know that if they had any cancellations before the 26th of September that I would be pleased to fill the openings. They were gracious but unfortunately no such luck. So I waited my turn like a good patient and finally the 26th had come. Once again, the final amalgam removal went quite well. I felt almost no reaction to removal initially and missed no time from work. About a week later my lower back started to hurt, so I took a good sauna and increased my kidney cleansing botanical blend dosage and the discomfort quickly went away. This process of mercury detoxification will go on for some time but I seem to be getting better every day.

Well throughout this process, I had stayed in touch with Dawne and had become very interested in the MSA machine. I just knew that I had to have one so that I could assist others the same as Dawne had done for me. So in the early part of August, I began making provisions to come up with the necessary funds to purchase the machine and all other necessary equipment and training. Well on October 3rd I did it. I purchased the MSA-21 from BioMeridian and followed up the purchase with three training sessions. The first session was a basic training course with BioMeridian in Utah. Next, I attended a seminar in Georgia. Finally, I also started a three year program with the Academy of Bio-Energetics, in Springfield, Missouri. These training sessions were instrumental in helping me to get started and be prepared to utilize the system. I practiced my skills for the rest of the year and started seeing clients with the MSA system at the end of 2001.

Again in early 2002, I hit a leveling off healthwise and wasn't sure what to do. But as my skills improved with the EAV system, I was able to detect an imbalance in my adrenal meridian and my gastrointestinal tract continued to hold my progress down. With the use of my system I found a couple of balancing remedies made by a company called NutriWest. These products were called Total Leaky Gut and DSF Formula. Total Leaky Gut was very helpful for my gastrointestinal problems and DSF Formula is a gladular/nutritional product which helped to revive my adrenal weakness. Within a week, I began to feel like my old self again and was starting to live my life somewhat like I did before the illness occurred. Over the next couple of months my progress was steady. I was now having even fewer bad days. While my diet was still quite limited, a great deal of my strength returned as was evidenced by my ability to lift heavier weights when working out at the health club. To say the least, I was ecstatic with my latest progress. As time progresses, I get healthier and my energy levels continue to increase, enabling me to experience each day with renewed strength and vigor. As my health improves, I continue to find evidence of viral and bacterial residue in my system, with my MSA. As I detoxify and heal my body of these toxins, my health continues to reach new levels of wellness to which I have not experienced in many years. This is likely the same pattern that those with auto-immune type of ailments will also have to experience if they wish to get well. In spite of the inconviences associated with healing, it was nothing compared to the shear misery I endured prior to using a holistic healing approach.

Clearly if I had made certain choices early on in my life many of my problems could have been averted. Most prominently, I would not have had any root canals or had any mercury amalgams placed in my mouth. This is especially true with my propensity to allergies and gastrointestinal disturbances. To say the least this would have saved me much time and grief. In spite of my difficulties, I harbor no ill will or feelings to those physicians who improperly diagnosed and/or treated me. For they were only doing the best that they could with the level of knowledge that they possessed at the time. Instead, I would rather be part of a movement which strives to unite western orthodox medicine and nutritionally based holistic approaches. In this way, we could have available a more complete array of healing modalities to address a diverse variety of health problems and imbalances. While both orthodox medicine and nutritionally-oriented holistic approaches have somewhat different roles they are equally crucial elements of the healing process.

In general terms, holistic healing methods are best used to address recurring or persistent problems. Whereas, western orthodox medicine is typically best suited when treating problems of an acute nature. Nutritionally based approaches are effective in helping to resolve recurring illnesses because they tend to address the individual's overall environment and lifestyle. Properly used, they can assist you in clearly identifying all the different triggers and offenders that are harmful to your situation. Once recognized, we are then better able to avoid and remove the irritants from our external environment. This then enables the natural healing process to move much more swiftly and effectively without interruption.

Conversely, traditional western medicine allows well-trained medical professionals to quickly address countless acute ailments, which need immediate attention and would likely be unresponsive to natural approaches. This list includes but is not limited to bone fractures, burns, scarring, some bacterial infections, severe lacerations, heart attacks, organ failure, contusions, and a ruptured appendix. Competent medical care should thus never be replaced with a natural holistic approach. Instead, a wiser approach is to utilize a mixture of the two philosophies. Obviously, physicians who use a balance of both approaches possess a greater diversity in their arsenal to deal with chronic diseases. Otherwise, they sometimes just simply do not have enough tools to fully facilitate healing. To solve this plight, it is necessary that one form a three person alliance and relationship with a holistic nutritional consultant and a medical physician who has at least some basic nutritional knowledge. In this way, you will have at least three people, including yourself, who are working together with a single goal in mind, maximizing your quality of life.

If successful in restoring your health, you will find it necessary to maintain a healthy lifestyle. This will help prevent a recurrence or the development of other ailments. Not surprisingly, much of the best information can be obtained by studying the lifestyles of healthy people. Because when you examine the lives of vigorous people, it becomes very clear why they are so healthy. Strangely, many people never even think of this approach and instead continue to do more of what contributed to their illness. However, total success will only come when we use wellness strategies that bring long-term positive results. Which is why if you want to experience a robust existence, it is essential that you live like the world's healthiest people. In time, you just may get the same result, vibrant health.

The rest of this book is devoted to providing you the motivation and information necessary to do just that. So let's get going!

Christopher K. Sembera (BS, CNC, Be.P)

CHAPTER 2
HEALTH BUILDING QUALITIES

There is much truth in the saying, "Nothing succeeds like success."
Maxwell Maltz, M.D.

The purpose of this chapter is to name and discuss several qualities that I have found to be consistent among those individuals who have improved their health and well-being. It is my view that one of the key reasons for their success is because they possessed or obtained a key group of qualities which enabled them to effectively maintain a strong focus of what is most important. These individuals then find themselves in a frame of mind which encourages them to accept a significant role in improving their health. This insight then enables them to look for potential solutions to their health problems. Health building people are also more skilled in developing an effective approach, to effectively fight through the obstacles that they will inevitable encounter along their journey.

Simply stated, developing a clear and aggressive mental approach of how to handle our situation is essential to overcoming the outside forces which otherwise can prevent success. Thus, if we are truly serious about improving our health situation, we too should utilize the upcoming clarity enhancing tactics.

To assist you in this task, I have compiled eleven elements which I am convinced are necessary for establishing the qualities for developing a properly focused mindset. In so doing, you will then be able to dramatically increase your chances of achieving your optimum state of wellness.

OPEN MIND

Having an open mind is the first step to making any improvements in one's life. This is true because before we can put new ideas and philosophies to use, we must first be open to the possibility that they can work. For when you go into a situation with your mind already convinced that some new approach will not work, you prevent yourself from learning a new option that may be of value. Simply stated, to determine if an approach can be helpful to your situation, you must be willing to evaluate its potential effectiveness. It is my recommendation that when encountering new information, you take several steps to determine if it is a fundamentally sound approach. This requires that you (1) thoroughly research the strategy; (2) ask yourself if it makes sense; and (3) conclude whether it is or is not a workable solution for your condition. If it meets all of these criteria, then consider giving it a try. You will find that when you evaluate nutritionally-based healing methods in this way, they will make great sense. However, if you have instead already made up your mind against these strategies, you may eliminate a tremendous opportunity for healing. Thus, it behooves us to wholly examine each approach with an inquisitive, open mind.

FORM A PARTNERSHIP WITH YOUR PHYSICIAN

Another strategy that health building people find essential is to develop a partnership with their physician. These folks usually find this step to be indispensable, because it enables them to work together with their doctor as part of a health reviving team. Forming a partnership also allows and encourages the individual to: (1) actively participate in their choice of treatment and strategy; (2) helps to give patients more control of the direction of their health plan; and (3) places both the patient and physician on the same wavelength. All three of these ingredients are required if you are to derive the full benefits of your medical consultations. However, before you can develop this type of relationship with your doctor, it is imperative that you first choose the correct physician. In my search for the ideal physician, I used three crucial qualifying factors to determine my selection. I wanted to find a physician that had: (1) an open mind to nutritionally based natural healing approaches; (2) an eagerness to learn about natural healing modalities; and (3) a willingness to listen to my concerns and help me make well-informed decisions. You can set your own criteria for selecting a physician or you can use mine. Regardless of what criteria you use, once you find your ideal physician, you will have a powerful ally guiding you to the best approach for your particular situation.

Christopher K. Sembera (BS, CNC, Be.P)

TAKE MORE RESPONSIBILITY FOR YOUR LIFE AND HEALTH

Taking more responsibility for your life and health are absolutely essential if you want to benefit fully from a wellness program. Yet, lack of personal responsibility has become rampant in our society, with individuals continuously attempting to pass blame for their problems onto someone else. Instead, we must take the necessary steps toward living healthful, well-balanced lives.

Furthermore, it is unfair of us to place the responsibility of our health totally in the hands of a doctor or health care professional, who we see just a few minutes upon each visit. If we are truly serious about healing our lives, then we must face the fact that this responsibility is ours. Before I lived this principle, I would constantly use medicines for every ache and pain to which my body would succumb. However, no magic wand or elixir exists for healing the chronic health disorders that afflict this world. Instead, we should closely examine and study what healthy individuals are consistently doing and then consider implementing those habits into our own lifestyles.

In reality, each of us has a tremendous healing power within ourselves. We just simply do not utilize this ability and expect instant results from the so-called wonder drugs. Yet no drug can hope to match the natural healing power of the human body; for all therapies are useless if the body, mind, and spirit do not repair themselves after treatment. Moreover, by building complete wellness we are able to prevent many potential health problems before they can occur.

For me, eating processed foods, drinking alcohol, and continuing my previous lifestyle were not as important as improving my health. You will also need to decide what is of greater importance to you, good long-term health or continuing your current way of life. The good news is that if you choose to make this positive self-commitment, your future can be transformed helping you to achieve wholeness.

SELF-ANALYSIS WITHOUT JUDGMENT

Another quality which health builders possess is the ability to evaluate their lifestyles without imposing harsh self-judgments. This is a crucial step. Because if we cannot examine ourselves and determine what areas of our life can be improved, then true health and happiness are unattainable. The truth is that we all play some role in our situation in this life. Hence, if we want to solve our problems, we must first become aware of the things that we already do well and where we need to improve.

Unfortunately, when self-analyzing, most of us get defensive and feel as though we are being forced to re-experience our failures. The difficulty here is that we are forced to review just how some of our previous actions have contributed to our current situation. In the initial phases of self-analysis, this can lead the individual to engage in self-blame. This is to be expected in the beginning stages of this self-evaluation. However, the key to effective utilization of this skill is to give our internal judge a vacation. We need not feel guilty about our previous actions, instead realize that life is a process of growth, and it is our job to learn from our experiences and make improvements as we go along. You can bet that this is exactly what health building people and those who have healed themselves have done. These individuals are simply better able to view their past mistakes, learn from them, and make the necessary modifications to help improve their situation. Not judging our past behavior is a secret of all those who have healed, for they know that they cannot change the past, but they can and do improve their future.

FIND A PURPOSE FOR YOUR CRISIS

Another factor that empowers people to make improvements in their lives is their ability to find a reason for their predicament. In general, most survivors learn to see their situation as an opportunity for personal growth. This can be a chance for building confidence, establishing priorities, growing spiritually, renewing friendships, improving health, advancing career goals, and ending toxic relationships. All of these are important elements for restoring and maintaining wholeness, and should be addressed concerning your situation. However, before you can rebuild your health, you need to learn what purpose, if any, your crisis is attempting to serve. This is necessary because I am of the opinion that one aspect of most chronic illnesses is actually our inner-self calling for its needs to be satisfied. To do this effectively, we must question ourselves to determine exactly what are our needs. Questions that you should ask yourself include: Why do I need this crisis? What need is this sickness trying to draw attention to? What area of my life is not being fulfilled? Truthful answers to these questions can provide tremendous insight into your inner being and what is needed to reestablish your wholeness. Although this type of self-questioning can be difficult, it is an important element for overcoming many crisis situations.

YOUR RIGHT TO MAKE MISTAKES

It is my assertion that one of the greatest mistakes a man can make is to be afraid to make one. Yet, many people in our society currently view mistakes as failures. However, mistakes can also serve as tremendous educational experiences, which propel us to higher levels of self-development. This is because our setbacks often teach us how to do something more effectively. Thus, once we learn to turn our interpretation of a difficult situation into an educational experience, we will then be capable of gaining valuable knowledge which is required for success.

Regarding health matters, people who rebuild their health learn from their mistakes, and then willingly make the necessary lifestyle adjustments until they achieve the results they desire. The important thing to remember here is that the only way to learn is to try. Mistakes are inevitable so do not be afraid of them, instead learn from your gaffes and how they can be used to your advantage.

PERSEVERANCE

One of the biggest factors separating the successful from the non-successful in this world is perseverance. Yet, many people quit when they come across an obstacle standing between them and their goal. What they do not understand is that those obstacles are actually stepping stones designed to help aid them in achieving their goals.

This is important; because in order to reach any goal, you must first commit yourself to mastering all roadblocks in your path. Once done, your optimum level of health will be within your grasp.

The point here is simply that to heal you must stay the course until you achieve the results you desire. Thus, if you seek great health just keep on keeping on, or as Winston Churchill said, "Never ever give up."

LONG-TERM PERSPECTIVE

If I were to choose one difference in the way of thinking between the successful and non-successful, it would be that successful people possess long-term perspective, whereas, the unsuccessful are merely instant gratification seekers. The same difference is true of the vibrantly healthy and ill individuals. Healthy people are constantly thinking about all the long-term benefits they will gain from their healthy lifestyles. These individuals live for the future realizing that is where they will spend the rest of their lives. Far too many ill and sickly people are instead continuously looking for a quick easy cure to their health problems. Unfortunately, many of these individuals will waste the rest of their lives, waiting for a miracle cure that may never appear.

To our detriment this type of short-term thinking has become prevalent in our society. This would include unwanted pregnancies, alcohol and drug addictions, and the over consumption of refined sugar and fast foods. However, the right way of thinking is to accept the reality that quick, easy fixes will not fully address our circumstances. We must instead stick with the proven, time-honored principles of success. In so doing, we can begin to approach the long-term positive success that we so richly deserve.

LISTEN TO YOUR BODY

When functioning in an optimum state, the human body is truly a magnificent machine. Instinctively operating, it seeks to meet all of its physical, emotional, and spiritual needs. Yet, modern living often moves us further and further away from nature. This type of lifestyle can be evidenced by noting the excessive use of refined foods, food additives, and continuous covering up of symptoms (warning signals) with stimulants or drugs.

Symptoms of illness serve to notify us that our body is out of balance and not functioning optimally. In actuality, they are a good thing alerting us that a problem exists. When illness, disease, or discomfort continue, it is vital that we, with the help of a physician and nutritional consultant, check and determine its cause. In so doing, we should be able to discover and address the origin of disease. This step is vital because it reminds us that drugs frequently do not fully address the underlying causes of the problem; they instead can cover or mask the symptoms of disease. Obviously, when used properly, drugs are a very helpful tool which medical professionals use to stimulate healing. What I am referring to is America's excessive use of drugs rather than placing emphasis on healthy balanced living.

In conclusion, listening to the signals that your body sends can supply you with a great deal of information about your overall state of health. Remember though that when symptoms of discomfort surface, your body is merely asking that you make improvements in your lifestyle, which is designed to meet all of your needs. Unfortunately, failure to maintain a healthy lifestyle often leads to the opposite — a lifetime of needless suffering and misery.

SUPPORT GROUPS

According to my experience, gathering with people who are striving to improve their health status is another significant part of health building. One reason for this is that people living with similar difficulties are usually more able to understand our situation. This will provide us with the opportunity to communicate with someone who knows firsthand exactly what we are experiencing. People can then see that they are not alone and become more capable of handling their situation.

Another benefit of a support group is that you can accumulate a wealth of ideas and information about dealing with your specific problem. This includes sharing information about physicians, new nutritional studies or products, personal experiences, and anything that could be beneficial to the members of the group. Frankly stated, we learn so much from each other in this type of setting that its importance cannot be measured.

During my journey, I had the wonderful opportunity to be a member of two such groups: the Human Ecology Action League of Central New York and cfsn.com. (HEAL is a national support group for those with allergies, multiple chemical sensitivities, and environmental illnesses.) (cfsn.com is a website which educates people on the process of heavy metal detoxification.) Both organizations are a tremendous source for information. Likewise, most of the individuals that these groups attract are highly motivated and constantly seeking more knowledge on how they can improve their quality of life. In my opinion, these are the very types of people with which you should try to associate.

For these reasons, I highly recommend that if you have the opportunity to become involved with this type of group that you do so. In so doing, you will be creating a network of support which can aid you through the healing process.

KNOWLEDGE

Knowing what to do is essential to success in any endeavor. Yet, we as a nation have developed a self-inflicted allergy to our greatest source of knowledge—books. This disturbs me greatly because the only way you are going to obtain all the information needed for achieving peak health is to read books on health and healing. A reasonable goal would be to read between 3 to 5 books on wellness. Of course, your situation may demand that you read significantly more publications to sufficiently educate yourself on your particular health problem. It all depends upon your situation and the degree of commitment that you are willing to make.

In Conclusion

According to my experience, these eleven values and strategies are common among those individuals who have improved their health. Therefore, it makes sense that if you want to enhance your health that you too should internalize these qualities. In so doing, you will be capable of laying the necessary groundwork required for healing.

CHAPTER 3
SELF - DESTRUCTIVE QUALITIES

*The next time you are sick or injured,
give your body credit for being able to heal.
Dr. Wayne Dyer*

The purpose of this chapter is to discuss the top nine characteristics of people who in my view are unprepared to improve their health. These folks are not ready to heal because they possess some or all of the self-destructive habits, qualities, and perceptions, which are disruptive to the healing process. However, by becoming knowledgeable of these pitfalls, people are more able to avoid these health-inhibiting roadblocks. This is absolutely necessary, because to combat ill health we must realize that people who possess these qualities greatly reduce their chances of recovery. It is therefore essential that you eliminate the following destructive qualities from your life.

PREJUDICES

Prejudice is a quality that harms oneself as well as others. The mere act of carrying around unpleasant feelings for certain groups of people causes us to waste time and energy creating negative thoughts. This, in turn, takes away valuable minutes which could have been spent on positive healing thoughts. The simple truth is that there is only so much time in the day, and it is imperative that we spend it on those things that assist us in the achievement of our positive goals. Once we replace intolerant negative thoughts with positive ones, we become more able to learn from all groups of people. In so doing, we will have greater access to additional information which may be beneficial to us and our health goals. If you seek health and success, it is strongly suggested that you work to remove all prejudice contained within your mind.

Christopher K. Sembera (BS, CNC, Be.P)

RATIONALIZATION

Another unproductive behavior is rationalization. This is simply the excuse individuals use to make an argument for continuing to eat and live in an unhealthy manner. Examples of some common rationalizations are:

"I ate the **entire** box of candy because I did not have enough room in my pantry;" or "I did not exercise today because I overslept and it would have been inconvenient later."

As you can easily imagine, these excuses tend to have very detrimental effects on our ability to adhere to a health-advancing plan. Therefore, it is of paramount importance that you not allow yourself to use these destructive traps. Instead, it is recommended that you consistently employ proven wellness building strategies. In so doing, you will then be moving in the direction of your quest for vibrant wellness.

HOLDING ONTO PAST EMOTIONS

Practically everyone has endured some of lifes' tough times, and as a result carries around heavy emotional baggage. This is very damaging to health and well-being. While damage left from past abuse has different levels of severity, all of it negatively affects health. Examples of past wounds include molestation, rape, an abusive relationship, or being the recipient of conditional love. As a result of experiencing these harsh situations, people often develop difficulties such as low self-esteem, lack of confidence, drinking to excess, poor spiritual development, eating disorders, and excessive gambling. These problems must be addressed so that we can release any leftover emotional residue and move on with our lives. Failure to do so will likely leave these individuals floundering in sorrow or repeatedly engaging in self-destructive behavior.

To resolve this mess, we need to forgive others for any past misdeeds which they have done to us, while at the same time preventing any future abuses from occurring. This should enable us to remove the emotional barriers which are blocking our path to success. If we are unable to do so, we will likely find ourseves without the ability to break the destructive pattern which we have fallen into and come to grips with our past. This should enable us to learn from our difficulties and use them as building blocks toward our own self-development.

PROCRASTINATION

Procrastination is one of the more common reasons that people miss their goal rather than heal. Typically, we fall short not because we are incapable of healing, but because we simply avoid starting a health-boosting program. A procrastinator will say, "I will start my healthy living plan after my exams." "Once the holidays are over, I'll start eating healthy." "I had planned to start the health regimen tomorrow but instead I'm going out of town."

Unfortunately, that tomorrow never comes for many people who foolishly waste time on tasks which bring no long-term positive results. If your health is important to you then get started immediately and do something each and every day to keep you mentally focused on your wellness goals.

FEAR OF FAILURE

One of the main reasons for procrastination is our next factor, the fear of failure. Due to this emotion, many people will not make a complete attempt to achieve their goals. However, it is important to note that most people who overcome chronic or recurring illnesses do so by learning what to do from a number of previously unsuccessful attempts. The sad thing here is that most people who make no effort to rebuild their health continue to carry around feelings of failure. Yet, when we engage in the pursuit of our aspirations and use proven strategies over an extended period, we frequently succeed. It is therefore strongly recommended that you work through your fears, rather than being shackled by them.

BLAMING OTHERS FOR YOUR SITUATION

Even though many people with health disorders were misinformed about health- building strategies, consistently blaming your poor health on others is of absolutely no benefit. It is instead an effective way of avoiding wellness, because it encourages the growth of a very negative viewpoint. Incessant blaming is also a time-wasting activity that prevents people from spending time and energy on healing activities. For this reason, it is best that you not spend too much time denouncing others and instead focus on finding solutions to your woes. Of course, one key to uncovering the answers to your problem requires that you look thoroughly within yourself. This can lead to an abundance of strategies for achieving your ultimate level of wellness.

WANTING SOMETHING FOR NOTHING

Another common destructive attitude is the desire of wanting something for nothing. Yet, success in virtually every endeavor always takes preparation. While the longing of wanting something for nothing is probably within all of us, nature requires that you earn your rewards. As you might suspect, healing and health preservation are also most effectively achieved with good, old-fashioned, hard work. There seems to be no way of getting around this time-honored principle. For this reason, it is wise that we follow through with all of the tasks that are required for building and maintaining an optimally functioning body, mind, and spirit.

ADDICTIONS

Rather than facing their problems, many people have unfortunately developed addictions to a wide number of substances. However, these compulsions tear them down physically, emotionally, and spiritually, eliminating their desire for total health. In reality, these individuals have lost control of their lives and created very distorted perceptions of their surrounding environment. The result is that their entire lives revolve around satisfying their cravings, leaving them with little or no time for the truly meaningful things in life. Nonetheless, the addict knows that their addiction is not in their best interest and therefore, has a very devastating effect on their self-esteem. In spite of this destructive cycle, addicts who seek help can beat this destructive pattern and regain control of their lives.

SELF-PITY

Everyone goes through periods of sorrow, especially during times of crisis. Yet, if self-pity becomes a permanent or ongoing attitude, improving your health situation becomes next to impossible. This is true because when we continue to dwell on our own difficulties, we tend to create insurmountable mental obstructions that stop us from even trying. Rather than feeling sorry for yourself, I suggest that you learn to appreciate all the good things that you have. This approach will be much more beneficial in helping you adhere to your health-building plan.

In Conclusion

Although, there are other thoughts and qualities that reduce our personal power, these nine seem to sum up the entire self-destructive mind-set. It is your job to make certain that your positive characteristics overwhelm and dominate these destructive qualities. Doing so will enable you to evolve into the person you were meant to become.

CHAPTER 4
EVERYTHING COUNTS

*Sickness and unhappiness are nature's way of urging us to
adopt a proper diet and way of life...*
Michio Kushi

Many people have lost recognition of the fact that they are their most valuable asset. This misinterpretation allows us to deviate from our own best interests and insufficiently meet the various requirements of our body, mind, and spirit. If this occurs, then a multitude of imbalances can materialize, leaving the individual extremely vulnerable to any inherent weaknesses. In contrast, when we possess total harmony between our body, mind, and spirit, achieving virtually anything is possible.

To attain this type of ideal balance, we must continually make a sufficient number of positive investments in ourselves. Our life is similar to one huge ledger and every action in which we engage is either beneficial or detrimental. This includes everything that we eat and drink, our thoughts, the people with whom we associate, our level of physical activity, and the information with which we arm ourselves. Thus, if we perpetually engage in a diverse blend of advantageous activities, we should be able to meet our needs and evolve into a healthy, happy person.

Unfortunately though, many people treat their automobiles and other possessions with more care than they do themselves. What these people do not realize is that their body, mind, and spirit are their vehicles for life. Thus, it is crucial that all three components of the individual be properly nourished. This can be done by satisfying our personal needs as listed in the ten factors of health and happiness.

The Ten Factors Of Health & Happiness

These are the required elements of health and happiness. The main objective of this program is to help you attain and maintain a proper balance of these factors in your life. When this is done, you will find yourself much more able to effectively control your physical, mental, and spiritual well-being. This approach provides an opportunity for healing because it empowers you with the ability to meet all key needs required to improve and preserve your wholeness. When we fail to satisfy each of these required elements, some very unhealthy imbalances will likely surface. For this reason, it is essential that you address sufficiently all of the above named factors. The following chapters are designed to help you achieve this task. So let's begin the journey with the very first step necessary for starting this process—prioritizing.

Christopher K. Sembera (BS, CNC, Be.P)

CHAPTER 5
PRIORITIZING

You say your life is overcrowded? I say, straighten out your priorities.
John A. McDougall, M.D.

    Before, starting any health building regimen, it is necessary to first determine and list your top priorities. Prioritizing, as used in this book, is the act of planning your life in accordance with your values. Properly applied, it is a powerful tactic that can help you recognize and then satisfy your personal needs. The reason prioritizing works is because it enables us to establish our own values system. As a result, we become empowered with the ability to see clearly the aspects of our life that bring us the most joy. We then become more able to spend time on those things that fulfill our values. Sounds simple, yet, most people claim they are too busy and do not have the time to prioritize their lives. Consequently, they typically end up spending little if any time on the very things that they claim are most important to them. This usually leads to a life of aimless wandering, resulting in the creation of an individual who never realizes the peace of mind and happiness that he or she so desperately seeks. Sadly, this happens far too often in modern civilization, where the tendency is to overemphasize things of material value or social power. Similarly, many people find that after achieving fame and material possessions, that those accomplishments fail to bring them the peace and happiness they expected. Instead, they often feel unfulfilled and incomplete, wondering what is missing from their lives. Whenever this occurs, it is a clear indication that your life is not in alignment with your values.

    Fortunately, once we make the commitment and take the time to set our priorities, it becomes very obvious how we are contributing to our feelings of sorrow and separation. This was certainly true for me. By clarifying my values, I was able to see exactly where I could enhance my life in areas that I previously had neglected. The sad truth of my case was that I was spending little time on many of the things which were most important to me. The shuffle of daily living was pulling me away from the important things like spiritual growth, peace of mind and health. Instead, I was wasting time working in a job that paid well but rapidly grew tiresome. Then, after the work day, I would typically seek instant gratification from alcohol and sugar. Does it sound familiar? As you might imagine, these quick-fixes eventually led to imbalances forcing me to take a long, hard look at the way I was living my life. The result of my internal analysis was the creation of my list of priorities, which is given below in their order of importance to me.

MY VALUES

1. My relationship with God. (Spiritual growth.)
2. Good Health. (Physical fitness.)
3. Happiness. (Optimistic state of mind.)
4. Peace of mind. (Being true to yourself.)
5. Relationships with opposite sex, family, and friends. (Love of others.)
6. Meaningful career.
7. Home and material possessions.
8. Education.
9. Financial security.
10. Hobbies. (Recreation.)

Beyond a doubt, my spiritual development was the most important factor that contributed to my restoration. By citing God as my top priority, all of my other values seemed to fall in place naturally. I believe the reason for this is because God lovingly guides each of us to the things that bring us the most joy. For me, prioritizing my life around God helps prepare me for all the problems that I will inevitably encounter in this life. Likewise, I also know that no matter how bad the situation, God will be by my side and provide whatever is necessary to help me deal with the circumstances. I recommend that you also keep spiritual development as your number one priority, which should of course be followed by good health.

Now it is time for you to select your top ten values. To start, I recommend that you should read over the entire list of values below and determine which ones you value most highly. Then, choose your top ten values, prioritizing them from 1-10 according to their importance. The purpose here is to assist you in putting your priorities into their proper perspective. You will then use this list to help structure more of your time around the things that you value most. However, just remember that all of these values are important and what you are actually striving for here is balance. You are just striving to place a little more emphasis on your key priorities.

YOUR VALUES

_____ Spiritual Growth
_____ Peace of mind
_____ Education
_____ Good Health
_____ Happiness
_____ Meaningful career
_____ Material possessions
_____ Hobbies
_____ Financial security
_____ Family
_____ Friends
_____ Giving to and sharing with others
_____ A close relationship with mate/spouse
_____ Others _____

Congratulations! Completing this initial step may be the most important thing that you will ever do because it distinctly shows where your priorities lie. So make certain that you take the necessary time to thoughtfully complete your list. It will be very beneficial toward helping you meet all of your needs, thus empowering you with the ability to dramatically improve your quality of life.

CHAPTER 6
SPIRITUAL-GROWTH

"When Christ rules your life completely, all negative things fade away and you gain the health of mind and body that God expects you to have"...Albert E. Clife

If you are truly serious about healing, spiritual growth is the most important health factor that needs to be present. Our spiritual health has a strong and vital impact on our physical and mental states. Many of the answers needed to address your health situation will be found in this aspect of your life. Before getting started, it is important that we clear up what I believe to be misconceptions about God including our relationship with the Creator, as well as our interactions with the spiritual realm.

Some people have the mistaken belief that the Creator is this oppressive Being who eagerly punishes those who dare to disobey the documented spiritual laws. However, God does not rule with an iron fist; God instead chooses to guide us to the things in life that make us happy. For the Creator is an all-loving, all-forgiving being who patiently waits for us to come back to our Father's unconditional love. God does this for everyone regardless of our past actions, by virtue of the Creator's desire to assist our spiritual development.

It is a fallacy that our ailments or mishaps in life are God's will. There is not a person on this planet who will ever convince me that God wills any of us to be sick or unhappy. It just does not make any sense to me that God would intentionally have us suffer. I instead believe that crisis situations are actually our spirit's way of signaling that its needs are not being satisfied. To meet its requirements, we must properly nourish ourselves with God's love; this is done through spiritual methods like prayer or meditation. Unfortunately though, far too many people have failed to prioritize their lives correctly and end up drifting away from their inner-most needs. However, when these spiritual needs are met, we become capable of tapping into our own health restoring energies.

Christopher K. Sembera (BS, CNC, Be.P)

The Spiritual World

Probably the most fascinating account of the spiritual world and how it relates to this life was given by Betty J. Eadie in her book *Embraced By The Light.* The story was based on her near-death experience, in which she claims to have visited and experienced heaven and the spiritual realm. According to Mrs. Eadie, before our spirits enter this world they actually choose many of the circumstances and situations that they will meet with while in their physical bodies. These choices can include one's health status, parents, and even many of the tragedies and misfortunes that we will experience. Our spirits willingly make these choices because coping with and overcoming life's many challenges provides great opportunities for growth.

If Eadie's depiction is accurate, it is important that we learn to use our difficulties in this life as occasions for personal development. In so doing, we can actually begin to turn our mishaps into opportunities for growth. As a result, we will likely develop an enhanced ability to solve our difficulties, and restore and maintain a healthy existence.

Spiritual Recession

Spiritual recession is a state of being that should be avoided at all costs. It refers to times when we deviate from what we know is in the best interest of our spiritual needs. Yet, humans are frequently attracted to and succumb to life's destructive forces. This in turn, has the effect of wearing us down and weakening our spirits. Situations like this generally arise when we get unnecessarily caught up in the pursuit of our earthly passions and aspirations. Damaging behavior varies greatly from person to person, however, the most common ones include excessive desire for fame, power, or material possessions, sex without love, unhealthy lifestyles and harboring negative emotions. These behaviors tend to leave us susceptible to disease and various states of unhappiness. Therefore, it is advised that we stay constantly focused on healing activities which will help to prevent a spiritual decline.

Love and Forgiveness

Crucial to healing is the utilization of **love and forgiveness**, because when these two healing tools are used, anything is possible. I believe that our spirits are composed almost entirely of love. Thus, to restore our spirit back to its ideal strength we need to love, love, love. For only by loving everyone and everything that God created, can we achieve total harmony between our body, mind, and spirit. To achieve this type of spiritual strength and balance, it is essential that we do nothing contradictory to this principle.

The other great healer is the offering of forgiveness. Unless we give complete forgiveness to each and everyone whom we feel has wronged us, a self-imposed barrier is placed between our physical body and our spirit. This barrier may then cause the healing process to come to a standstill. We only hurt ourselves when we retain negative emotions. Once we forgive those who have mistreated us, we can then demolish these roadblocks. Then and only then, will God and our spirit be ready to provide harmony and healing to our physical and mental existence.

To forgive effectively, it is vital to realize that we hurt ourselves by harboring this destructive energy. We would be better served by releasing others from our inner frustrations. My reasoning behind this comes from scripture, where we are warned that if we want to be forgiven that we must choose to forgive those that have offended us. Isn't it interesting how God switches the circumstances around and then allows us the opportunity to resolve our own problem through the act of forgiveness. This proves to me that God empowered us with the ability to tap into our own spiritual healing energies and expects us to use them.

Therefore, if we wish to stop the internal cycle of spiritual and emotional self-destruction, we must forgive. Although this can be a real chore, it is necessary if you are to find the inner comfort and peace required for healing.

Miracles

A discussion of miracles is necessary here, because of the existing flawed assumptions about them. Many people believe that in order for an occurrence to be a miracle some spectacular optical occurrence needs to transpire. This is likely due to all the phenomenal visual displays which are now commonplace in today's entertainment industry. Our visually stimulated society now expects miracles to manifest themselves in divine splendor that marvels the senses of all who behold them. Yet, according to *Webster's Vest Pocket Dictionary*, a miracle is merely an event that cannot be explained by known laws of nature. It does not require that brilliant images or spectacular events take place.

Many people also misinterpret the way that God works miracles. We typically expect God to use divine power to instantaneously heal all of our weaknesses and ailments. God rarely works this way. The Creator instead provides us with what is needed, then expects us to utilize our God-given abilities to solve our problems. This is significant because if God were to solve all of our problems quickly, we would then be cheated out of the internal growth that we would otherwise have gained from the crisis. Instead, the Creator tends to use more patient approaches to intervene in our lives. Methods used by God could include sending helpful people into our lives, leading us to self-help books and programs which assist us, as well as creating circumstances that inspire us to change. These are in my judgment all hidden miracles which God uses to help address our difficulties. Unfortunately, these shrouded miracles typically go by unrecognized.

How often have you been in need and someone or something comes into your life and offers assistance? Do you typically discount these happenings as mere coincidence? Or do you instead think someone up above is looking out for you? Your way of interpreting these incidents determines your understanding and belief in miracles. If you look at life believing that God is endlessly assisting you, then you will realize that we experience countless numbers of smaller, hidden miracles throughout our lives.

The Tools of Spiritual Enhancement

Your level of spiritual development is one of the factors that determines your state of health and well-being. This is true because our spirits are constantly in need of nourishment which can only be derived from spiritual enhancing activities. The five most common tools used for spiritual development are the application of effective prayer, meditation, listening to God's signals (our conscience), regularly attending church services, and working on your spiritual education. Consistently used, these spiritual enhancing techniques will assist you in the rediscovery of your internal healing energies, which are required for total health.

Prayer

The act of praying is one of the first things that spiritually conscious people learn. It is the most frequently used method for communicating with God. Prayer can be employed in a wide variety of ways including asking for God's intervention, seeking forgiveness, or just thanking God for all of our divine blessings. The reason that prayers are so effective is because God always answers our prayers in the most skillful way needed to help us reach our next level of growth. He does this by sending us everything and everyone we need to handle the obstacles that we will inevitably encounter. Progress is often slow and tedious, nonetheless, it is absolutely necessary that this development take place for us to reach our next level of spirituality.

To increase the effectiveness of our prayers, we must confidently express faith in the Almighty. In prayer, discuss with God what we desire (although God already knows) and then thank the Creator in advance for making it happen. This demonstrates that we have a great deal of faith and believe that God will help our cause. As the late renowned author and minister, Norman Vincent Peale wrote, "Always remember you will receive as a result of prayer exactly what you think, not what you say." Far too many of us ask for God's assistance then mistakenly question whether our prayers will be answered. The doubts that we maintain exemplify our lack of faith and hinder us from advancing. In my opinion, this occurs because God will usually only help us according to the degree of faith that we possess. Therefore, it is essential that God allow this growth process to continue, for we will then have the opportunity to benefit from our experiences. Otherwise, God would be cheating our spirits out of a great opportunity for growth.

Christopher K. Sembera (BS, CNC, Be.P)

I am also convinced that prayers should come from the heart rather than repetitiously out of some prayer book. One's own prayers require more thought, causing us to look more deeply within ourselves and our lives. Plus these prayers will be more passion-filled, which may encourage a more rapid and powerful response. You will also save God from having to listen to the same prayers over and over again!

Besides self-prayers, you can also benefit greatly from the prayers of others. To prove this, a study in the mid 1990's was designed by cardiologist Randolph Byrd to determine scientifically what healing effects, if any, were to be derived from prayer. Over a ten-month period, 393 patients were admitted to the coronary care unit at San Francisco General Hospital. The patients were put into two separate groups; one group was being prayed for while the other was not. This double-blind study found several interesting differences between the two groups. *Natural Health's* March/April 1994 issue reports that the patients who received prayers,

- were five times less likely than the unremembered patients to require antibiotics;
- were 3 times less likely to develop pulmonary edema, a condition in which lungs become filled with fluid due to a poorly functioning heart;
- did not require endotracheal intubation, although 12 in the unprayed for group required this procedure.

This evidence supports the theory that prayer aids in healing. Therefore it is wise when a crisis occurs, to request the prayers of others, especially from family members and friends who have strong emotional ties to us.

The Bible also discusses the power of shared prayer and how beneficial it can be. In Matthew 18:19, Jesus remarked about the power of united prayer, "Again I tell you, if two of you join your voices on earth to pray for anything whatever, it shall be granted you by my Father in heaven." The key points here are, (1) that two or more people gather in one place, and (2) that the individuals harmoniously desire the same goal. When this is done, miracles can begin to happen.

Of course, it is still extremely effective to pray alone, because it is during these silent reflective states in which we meet one on one with God. For optimum effectiveness, it is recommended that you set aside a minimum of 10-15 minutes each day for quiet prayer. Doing so will replenish your spirit with the enlightenment and strength it needs for healing. Of course, you can also pray whenever you are in need of God's guidance, for the Creator is always there to give us exactly what we need.

Meditation

Another powerful tactic used to aid spiritual growth is meditation. It can be adapted to serve a number of purposes such as relaxation, stress reduction, and internal problem-solving. In my view, its most effective role is its ability to aid us in communicating with our spirits and thus to reconnect with our internal spiritual energy. Tapping into this energy can provide tremendous healing power, which may then be channeled to address our needs. To benefit from meditation, it is essential that you go to a quiet place for about 10-15 minutes, relax your entire body, and breathe freely, so that you can relax and be alone with your thoughts. Doing so will enable you to examine and more deeply contemplate your situation.

Utilizing this process will give you the opportunity to examine a wide range of situations and circumstances. This could include determining the viability and logic behind a holistic healing approach, finding answers to various questions, and rebuilding your spiritual strength. Thus, this approach can be helpful to a whole host of problems.

If further information on meditation is desired, see Joan Borysenko's book *Minding the Body, Mending the Mind*. It is widely recognized as one of the most popular sources for details and information on the meditation process and its many benefits.

Listening To God (Our Conscience)

Our conscience is the communication instrument God uses to aid our growth and guide us through life. Utilizing this gift will enable us to maintain constant contact with God as to how we should live our life. It is crucial that we heed the messages sent to us through our inner consciousness. Although following the moral advice of our conscience is not always an easy thing to do, we will benefit by adhering to its recommendations. We gain from this process because God uses our conscience to inform us as to which life choices will assist our long-term best interests. My personal experiences can certainly confirm this point. When I follow the recommendations of my conscience, I typically make very wise decisions. Straying from the advice of my inner awareness usually leads to poor choices and unwanted consequences. If we are to grow closer to God and successfully address our circumstances, it is imperative that we follow the guidance of our conscience.

Attending Worship Services

To me, Mass is like a pep-rally for the soul. These services have the ability to stir up strong passions and touch us in ways which inspire us to become better people. In order for us to gain from religious services, it is essential that we be both attentive and open to the teachings of our Father. This will expose us to God's message as well as the priest's interpretation of how God's teachings relate to our everyday lives. Both elements remind us of our spiritual needs and steer us away from the trivial things in life which interfere with our spiritual development. I strongly recommend that you attend worship services and receive the spiritual support required to keep your life headed on the right path.

Spiritual Education

Many embark on deeper levels of spiritual instruction. This is typically done through a diverse number of approaches which include taking religious and theology courses, reading books on spiritual development, attending religious retreats or participating in Bible study groups. All of these enable individuals to gain valuable insight into God's teachings and to acquire extensive spiritual wisdom.

The initial exposure to spiritual education for many of us was when we attended parochial schools. As you probably know these religious schools require their students to take theology or religion courses. Therefore, these students have considerable access to some type of moralistic philosophy. This exposure gives them a prime opportunity to develop a close relationship with God, as well as learning right from wrong. Undoubtedly, these individuals have a definite advantage over those who attend schools without spiritual instruction. For this reason, I strongly suggest that if you have the opportunity to attend a faith based school that you do so.

    The next educational tool used by many people to gain spiritual knowledge is reading spiritually enhancing books. These particular publications are excellent tools for learning what is expected of us and how we can grow closer to God. Obviously the best book for this purpose is the Bible. However, many other excellent books on spiritual growth have also been written. Some of my favorites are *Life's Not Fair But God Is Good*, by Dr. Robert Schuller, *Let Go and Let God* by Albert E. Clife, *Spiritual Crisis* by Meredith L. Young-Sowers, *A Closer Walk, A Spiritual Lifeline To God* by Catherine Marshall, *Never Alone* by Joseph F. Girzone, *Living Between Two Worlds* by Joel S. Goldsmith, and *Spiritual Growth* by Sanaya Roman. These works are interesting and packed with information which is designed to help answer most if not all of your questions. Obtaining these or any other corresponding publications is a powerful educational strategy that can easily be accessed at your local library or bookstore.

    For additional experiences and education, religious retreats and Bible study groups are available through various church groups. These two educational outlets generally involve lots of interaction with others who are also pursuing a closer relationship with God. Due to this, we can learn tremendously from these people, for they will be sharing their personal stories and beliefs about how God has positively impacted their lives. This will in turn, encourage us to review our own lives and recall times in which we believe God assisted us. Engaging in these and other educational activities inevitably helps to strengthen our faith, making us more confident to pursue our goals and aspirations. Consequently, this strategy will be tremendously advantageous to those seeking greater spiritual energy.

In Conclusion

The above strategies provide ideas of how you can attain your highest level of spirituality. You can use these or choose other approaches to develop this aspect of your life. However, you must commit yourself to growing closer to and incorporating God's messages into your life. For it is my conclusion that when we live in accordance with God's commandments, we generally find ourselves filled with love and happiness and better able to handle the difficulties associated with human life.

Key Points

1. **Love and forgiveness are the two greatest healing tools which humans possess.**
2. **Prayer and meditation are two of the most effective ways to converse with God.**
3. **Our conscience is God's way of guiding us through life.**
4. **Spiritual growth can be achieved in many ways including attending worship services, taking religious or theological courses, religious retreats, bible study groups, and reading spiritual books.**

CHAPTER 7
LOVE

Love offers itself as a continual feast to be nourished upon...Leo Buscaglia

Ultimately, the desire for all of us is to love and be loved; without it nothing else truly matters. In fact, much of what we do is meant to bring us toward this blissful mental state. To achieve this, people often make attempts at self-improvement through fitness, education or job training, and spiritual enhancement. Virtually all of these actions are done either to expand the love of God, self, or for the love and admiration of others. Yet in order for love to be fully realized, we must master the four different types of love. These types include: (1) our relationship with God, (2) self-esteem, (3) love of friends, family, and spouse, as well as, (4) the love of serving our spiritual brothers and sisters. Experiencing and utilizing all four types of love are crucial, because without them internal harmony cannot be fully attained.

First, of all everyone must have a loving relationship with God. This is indispensable because God's undying love for us is the most powerful and available love that exists for the human race. Each of us is very different about the way we express our love of God. Some are very vocal and open, while others have a more internal relationship. Your mode of love and expression makes little difference, only that you work to strengthen this relationship. To do so only requires that you learn more about God's undying love for us. For as I earlier stated, God loves us all unconditionally and is always there for us no matter how far we deviate from His love. In like manner, when we commit our lives to loving God, He enriches us in ways that we cannot possibly imagine. Unquestionably though, to love God we have to first believe in the existence of a higher power. If not, then you need far more assistance than this program can provide. My advice, start praying!

The next type of love requires that people respect and value themselves as their most precious asset. This is significant, because if you are lacking in self-love you may find it difficult even to start the process of healing. One of the likely reasons for this hesitancy is our feelings of inadequacy and unworthiness of the effort that is necessary for rejuvenation. To reverse this scenario all that is required is for you to start making positive investments in yourself. This is effective because the action steps you take to improve your current situation will also have a lasting beneficial impact on your self-esteem.

However, before we can begin this process, we must initially determine our current level of self-esteem. This can be evaluated by asking yourself a few simple questions. Who is the most important person in your life? Would it be your spouse, your kids, or your friends? You might be surprised to know that in actuality, none of these are correct. Instead, you should have stated that as far as you are concerned, you are the most important. Failure to cite yourself could be a signal that your self-esteem is not as high as it should be. Of course, this does not mean that you should disregard the needs of others, particularly when dealing with young children or ill family members. It is instead a core value which says that you must satisfy your needs over the needs, and especially the wants, of others. The reason for this is simply that you cannot possibly help others meet all of their needs if you are neglecting yours. It is therefore recommended that you first take the necessary steps to address your needs, then you will be more prepared to assist others in meeting theirs.

Another obstacle that many of us have to face is a tendency to pass very harsh judgments on ourselves. These self-evaluations can be brutal and oftentimes they negatively affect our psyche. According to self-esteem expert and author, Nathaniel Brandon, "Of all judgments that we pass in life none is as important as the one we pass on ourselves, for that judgment touches the very center of our existence." Instead of this approach, we need to give our internal judge a vacation and simply realize that we did the very best we could with the belief system we possessed earlier. Once we do this, we can be free to appreciate the things that we do well, plus, address the areas in our lives that need improving.

Before we can strengthen our weaknesses, we must first learn the root causes of low self-esteem and how it is developed. Sharon

Wegscheider-Cruse, author of *Learning to Love Yourself*, claims that it most commonly results when children are born to parents who are themselves lacking in self-confidence. Consequently, as these children age, they tend to develop low self-concepts. These individuals typically grow up harboring numerous negative feelings such as fear, guilt, envy, anger, and sorrow. Later in life, this can advance to more serious problems like eating disorders, alcoholism, and drug addiction. These destructive lifestyles tell their body and mind that they are not valuable, thus forming a false belief that they are undeserving of true love and happiness. It must be stated that it would be unfair to blame our parents for our problems, as they have done the best they could with the knowledge and financial means that they possessed. The point is to understand the cause of low self-esteem so that we can resolve it.

The next step required for augmenting our self-concept is choosing to center our thoughts on positive self-dialogue (positive affirmations). The reason that this is so important is because people who suffer with low self-esteem are continuously engaging in negative self-talk. Therefore, if we desire to raise our self-worth we need only do the opposite, which would be to engage in positive self-dialogue. Along with raising our self-concept, we may also experience more success in our lives, simply because people with high levels of self-esteem tend to lead healthier, happier, and more successful lives. Fundamentally stated, positive affirmations assist us in the achievement of our goals, while negative internal-dialogue prevents success. Therefore, it is to our advantage that we communicate with ourselves in a positive, encouraging manner.

As stated earlier, it is necessary for you to actively invest in yourself to improve your self-esteem. To do this it is essential that we be true to ourselves and our values, rather than the values of others. Amazingly, many times this is the most difficult step for people, because saying yes to your needs often means saying no to others. Although this may be difficult initially, it is absolutely necessary if you are to develop a healthy self-concept. By following through and saying yes to yourself, you will invariably spend more time on the things in life that you value most. What a powerful strategy! You focus on the things that you value, develop a plan on how you will work toward specific goals, and then follow through with positive action steps. This method prepares you to win. Moreover, as you succeed you feel better about yourself, thus raising your self-esteem through the roof.

Third, is love of your significant others, whether that be your friends, family, or that special person with whom you wish to spend the rest of your life. Spending lots of quality time with those whom we love is something everyone claims is of vital importance. However, many couples spend only a few minutes per day communicating with each other. Although couples are typically together much more than a few minutes, they are generally preoccupied with a number of activities. These distractions include amusements such as watching television, conversing on the telephone, or involvement in contrasting activities. Yet the sort of communication that is necessary is when we actively and completely engage in intimate conversation with our mate. This type of intense communication is essential if we are to develop and maintain a healthy relationship with our significant other. If people are only spending a few minutes per day communicating with the person of their dreams, is it any wonder that so many people have unfulfilling relationships? You can avoid this story line by simply spending quality time communicating with the one you love. In so doing, you will be setting yourself up to receive a steady supply of healing love.

Your friends and family also require that you unreservedly invest your time and energy in them. Remember, throughout your lifetime you will need the love and support of these people. This is especially true when life throws its inevitable curve balls like disease or crisis into your path. Therefore, do not hold in your love. Share it freely and unconditionally with the important people in your life. Or else, they may be unwilling to give you theirs when you need it most.

Lastly, we must be willing to provide loving service to all of God's children. To accomplish this objective, we must be willing to give, share, and return kindness to all others. Assisting others is not only a very rewarding experience, but it is also necessary if we are to flourish and grow. To achieve the highest level of fulfillment, humans must satisfy their need to help others. This is largely done by treating every person you come across the same way in which you want to be treated. In most cases, you will find that this will be a simple task, such as being nice to a busy cashier while waiting in line, or by simply listening to someone who is experiencing tough circumstances. However, it is important that you remember many problems or situations require more assistance than you can provide. When you find yourself in this situation, try to point these folks in the right direction and move on.

After providing assistance to individuals, it is necessary that we allow them the freedom to make their own choices, even if they are going to make the wrong ones. Although this can be difficult to watch, it is absolutely necessary that we allow people this freedom. There is nothing that educates people better than experiencing the consequences of their actions. In fact, allowing these situations to occur actually empowers people to grow from and take responsibility for their lives, rather than depend on someone else. However, if they desire your advice or recommendations, help whenever you are able. If people do not want your help then back off; you can assist them later if they so desire. Until then, stay focused on your goals and be ready to help whenever your assistance is wanted. Providing your service will be without a doubt, the most kind and loving thing that you can ever do for another human being. This will in turn come back to you, for we tend to get back what we give.

Conclusion

The key point to grasp from this chapter is that nothing is more important in life than the gift of love. Utilizing this blessing effectively requires that we love God, ourselves and all of God's children. For this reason, it is vital that we accept and build a healthy well-rounded supply of all four types of love. Once done, your life will be filled with more love and happiness than you ever imagined possible.

Key Points

1. **One key to happiness is a positive and loving relationship with God.**

2. Learn to value and love yourself.
3. Loving all others, especially your mate, is a necessary part of human happiness.
4. Contributing to and sharing with others is a valuable part of human development.

CHAPTER 8
POSITIVE ATTITUDE

These tough-minded optimists may be of average intelligence and looks, but they know how to keep themselves motivated, and they approach their problems with a can-do philosophy...
Alan Loy McGinnis

One thing is clear. A positive mental attitude is an absolute must for the individual striving for optimum health. A positive thinker will see all the potential benefits of living healthy and then find ways to implement health-enhancing techniques. In contrast, pessimistic individuals choose to ignore all the advantages and create an endless list of excuses why they cannot make improvements in their diet and lifestyle. This type of negative mind-set will make it very difficult to achieve wellness goals. Thus, it is essential that you avoid this cynical perspective and instead work to acquire and keep an optimistic frame of mind.

To help you with this task, I provide six attitude-enhancing strategies. Included in this list are: (1) expecting good things to occur, (2) reframing, (3) embracing obstacles, (4) visualization, (5) positive affirmations, and (6) associating with positive people. Business and salespeople have long touted these techniques as being effective for building an optimistic perspective. We too can use these proven tactics to assemble a confident disposition. Once done, you will be prepared to utilize the required health-building strategies and thus experience a far greater quality of life.

EXPECT GOOD THINGS TO OCCUR

Devoted users of this strategy are convinced that their thoughts can and do have profound physiological effects on their body and its resultant health. Their reasoning for this stance is that our subconscious mind has a tremendous ability to create exactly what we spend the majority of our time thinking about. This can relate to all areas of life: our career choice, financial situation, or even our health status. In terms of health, Bernie Seigel, M.D. claims that people who spend most of their lives expecting good things to occur get sick far less often. At the same time, he finds that those who worry excessively are more likely to develop some form of ill health. With this point in mind, it is clearly in our best interest to be optimistic about our futures. In so doing, we will be able to enhance our quality of health in the coming weeks, months, and years.

REFRAMING

Reframing is a tactic I came across while listening to Anthony Robbins' best-selling audiotape set, *Unlimited Power*. Robbins advises us to see the positive aspects in seemingly negative situations, so that we develop an optimistic perspective. This new cheery outlook should then help inspire us to seek out and find solutions to our problems.

A simple example could be a woman who has an allergic reaction after using a certain brand of makeup. Rather than becoming upset, she accepts her body's warning, and avoids future use of that particular brand of makeup.

Better yet, let's say you have a severe health problem. Instead of feeling sorry for yourself, you choose to learn the underlying cause(s) of these symptoms, and before long formulate a plan to overcome the problem. You then follow through with that plan until wellness is restored.

As these two examples show, reframing helps to put us in the right state of mind required for addressing the obstacles that we encounter. It then directs us toward competent solutions to our plight.

Now that you have been exposed to this attitude-raising tool, make certain that you put it to good use. You can rest assured that some form of reframing is used by all successful people, because everyone is faced with difficulties in their lives. Triumphant folks are just more effective at seeing the advantageous elements of each situation and then making adjustments in their lives to access those benefits. We too must learn to better detect and procure the beneficial aspects of difficult situations. In so doing, we will become better able to find and create solutions to our most complex challenges.

EMBRACE OBSTACLES

If you wish to maintain a positive mental outlook you need to accept that there will be obstacles between you and your goals. Embracing this fact not only helps you prepare for these hindrances, but can also put you in a mental state which enables you to use these experiences to your advantage. Obstacles are actually knowledge-building experiences which lead us to information helpful to overcoming our difficulties. Therefore, if we want to improve our situation, we must first remove all obstacles in our path.

For example, during my crisis I had numerous food allergies which were causing a multitude of symptoms. I decided to use this situation as an opportunity to learn about food allergies and what natural approaches could help address them. After much research, I chose to go on a rotational diet and over time was able to detect my food intolerances. This information helped me to make important adjustments in my diet. I was then able to structure my diet effectively around other well-tolerated foods which were nutritious and helpful to my health goals. In essence, learning to accept my problem as an opportunity for personal growth put me in a mental state that was conducive to finding a solution. If you want to overcome a prolonged illness, you must willingly do the same. It will enable you to persevere through the tough times and catapult you toward your optimum level of wholeness.

VISUALIZATION

This strategy can be one of the most powerful attitude-enhancing tools available. It is similar to daydreaming but with one significant difference. The distinction is that daydreaming is mental waste; whereas visualization is mental work. Visualization works by helping its user mentally experience an event or occurrence before it actually takes place. Regularly applied, it will greatly assist in building confidence and inner strength. As a result, visualization is employed by many of our most successful entertainers, athletes, and business people as a tool to improve their overall efficiency and effectiveness.

One person who acknowledged his use of this tactic is All-Pro National Football League kicker, Morten Andersen. In a September 1993, issue of the New Orleans *Times Picayune*, Mr. Andersen cited sports imagery (also known as visualization) as contributing to his success. Andersen said that he does not think of the negative. "I think I can make every kick I'm put out on the field to make. I don't want to walk out there scared, intimidated, or tentative. You've got to be aggressive, focused and locked in for every kick. That's what I prepare myself to do." Plainly stated, Mr. Andersen uses this tool to stay positive and improve his mental focus. You too can benefit from the application of this strategy, either for health-building or simply to help preserve wellness.

To make visualization work for you, just follow these three simple steps. **One, set a time of the day that you will use to visualize the attainment of your objective.** You can do this at night, in the morning, upon waking, or anytime that you find convenient. Make certain when selecting your time that you stick to it. This is important because those individuals who use this tool effectively tend to maintain a specific time for visualizing. In contrast, those who do not adhere to a definate time, typically fail to utilize this strategy.

Second, your visualization should include your personal environment and society reacting positively to the new optimum you. Imagine the people around you, and the positive remarks people will say to you. Imagine the expressions on their faces. Experiencing these positive images will likely cause your confidence level to grow, which is essential if you are going to perservere through the challenges which you will be facing.

The last key ingredient is to imagine yourself feeling the emotions you would experience after achieving your goal. If we can mentally experience peace of mind or any other positive emotional state, we dramatically enhance the effectiveness of this strategy. This works due to its ability to inspire our desire for reaching our goals. We also become more willing to adhere to the elements required for healing, which is of course necessary, if we are truly serious about achieving our objective.

A complete visualization could be as follows. Let us say that your goal is to fully restore your health. Then you would start by visualizing a clear mental picture of yourself in peak health. See and feel yourself having unlimited amounts of energy, being pain-free, no longer suffering from any affliction or symptoms. Next, imagine your body operating at optimum levels in all of its functions. Once you see yourself fully healed you should ask your awareness a few simple questions. Where you would go? Who would you go see? What clothes would you wear? To help make this experience even more vivid, add bright colors. Make the images larger or smaller. Have the people talk in odd voices, or if anyone has ever hurt you in the past have them apologize to you. How do these experiences make you feel? Are you happy or sad? Do you feel ten to twenty years younger? Routine use of this exercise nurtures your emotional development and puts you back in control of your life and destiny. The healing power that can be gained from this strategy is endless. But like anything else, to improve from this process you must regularly utilize it. If employed, visualization can help program your mentality for success in all of your pursuits.

POSITIVE AFFIRMATIONS

The chief aim of this tactic is to facilitate positive self-talk. Optimists are typically very effective at communicating positively with themselves, whereas negativists are constantly abusing themselves with destructive self-dialogue. This is important, because our thoughts, whether good or bad, tend to manifest themselves in our physical body. If you want to become a positive thinker, you must avoid negative internal conversations and instead provide optimistic confidence-building messages to yourself. Positive affirmations can thus play a vital role in dramatically improving our future.

Benefiting from affirmations requires that they **be personal, deal with the present, and be positive**. A simple example of this would be the four words, "I can do it." When we repeatedly state this phrase, it tends to exact a tremendous positive influence over our level of certitude. Positive affirmations can assist us in virtually any type of situation, like creating enthusiasm for your new healthy lifestyle or stimulating the healing process. Such affirmations would include optimistic phrases like: "I love exercise; I love eating nutritious foods; I feel stronger every day; I am getting healthier every day." These particular affirmations contain all three required elements and thus help us stay positive about bettering our current situation. They do this by sharpening our mental focus so that we can see and experience the emotional advantages of these cheerful phrases.

In my humble judgment, spiritual affirmations tend to be the most powerful. These affirmations possess added strength because of their potent ability to tap into our need for a spiritual connection with the Creator. My most trusted affirmations include Bible quotes like, "If God be with us, who can be against us;" and "if ye have faith nothing shall be impossible unto you."

Use of these spiritual affirmations helped me to stay optimistic throughout my period of recovery. They did this by providing my mind with inspirational messages. This tool can assist you as well. Just allow their meaning to penetrate your inner thoughts. The result will likely be a dramatic enhancement of your mental state, propelling you toward optimum wellness.

ASSOCIATE WITH OPTIMISTIC, SUPPORTIVE PEOPLE

The people in our environments have very infectious effects on our emotional states. Optimistic, supportive people help to elevate our moods and provide us with the encouragement to pursue our aspirations. Non-supportive, negative thinkers tend to pull us down emotionally and distract us from everything we try to accomplish. It is suggested that we surround ourselves with those who choose to see the positives in life. Thus, we will create a supportive atmosphere that will be conducive to meeting our goals.

Developing this type of healing environment requires that you first become the eternal optimist. If we are always in a positive, happy state then those who associate with us will be affected by our optimism. Our new cheerful outlook will also help to attract other positive, caring individuals into our lives. At the same time, the law of repulsion becomes so energized that negative, non-supportive people will be repelled by our incessant optimism.

This point can be easily seen by observing how we tend to be upbeat when around someone who is in a positive state. Likewise, have you noticed when you treat others kindly that they are inclined to respond favorably to you? Yet on days when you are emotionally downcast, the people around you also are apt to be disheartened. These scenarios provide proof that humans become very much like the people with whom they choose to associate. Optimists simply have the ability make those around them happier and more supportive.

Along with these six strategies, do not forget to laugh and smile, and do something nice for someone each day. Not only will this kindness give you an emotional lift but it also enhances the lives of those who choose to aid you along the way.

Conclusion

In summation, a positive mental attitude is an absolute necessity if you are striving to rebuild your health. If you learn to view the lifestyle changes that coincide with your healing program as improvements, you will likely be more able to adhere to your healing plan. As a result, you will have a far greater chance to improve or even solve your problem. What it comes down to is that the choice is yours. Optimism or pessimism; which will you select?

Key Factors

1. Develop an attitude of positive expectancy.
2. Use reframing to discover the positive element present in every seemingly bad situation.
3. Utilize visualization to enhance your effectiveness.
4. Create and utilize positive affirmations to build a more positive, confident you.
5. Surround yourself with positive people who want you to succeed.
6. Remember to laugh and smile each and every day.

Christopher K. Sembera (BS, CNC, Be.P)

CHAPTER 9
OPTIMUM EATING

Medicine is the study of disease, nutrition is the study of health...Adelle Davis.

Without question, following an optimum eating plan can dramatically improve one's quality of life. Sadly, far too many of us do not properly utilize this tool. To address this matter, I use this chapter to provide the necessary guidelines for an idealistic eating plan. If regularly followed, it can provide a vast number of benefits such as preserving excellent physical and mental health, improving one's skin tone, increasing energy levels, reducing premature aging and helping one establish and maintain their ideal weight. Included in this discussion are the reasons that inaccurate nutritional data exists, foods that are best avoided or limited, a description of unhealthy eating habits, as well as, the foods which help us achieve our optimum state of well-being. This information will enable you to make wiser food choices and structure your eating around foods which contain the most complete supply of nutrients. It will then be your responsibility to apply this knowledge and properly nourish yourself, so that you can reach your full health potential.

The Relevance of Nutrition

Throughout my research, I was repeatedly enlightened by nutritional health books like *The Yeast Connection*, by William Crook, M.D., *The Macrobiotic Way*, by Michio Kushi and *The E. I. Syndrome*, by Dr. Sherry A. Rogers. These, explain how and why nutrition plays such a major role in the prevention of disease and maintaining good health. I also came across several inspirational books written by individuals who had overcome cancer and other major illnesses through diet and lifestyle enhancements. Three of my personal favorites are *Recovery from Cancer*, by Elaine Nussbaum, *Recalled by Life*, by Anthony Sattilaro, M.D., and Tom Monte, and *Confessions of A Kamikaze Cowboy* by Dirk Benedict. All three provide an incredible amount of encouragement, which can help motivate you through the inevitable tough times associated with conquering ill health. There are countless other existing health-related books which cite tests, reports, or other fascinating stories of people overcoming debilitating symptoms and ailments. Not only did these folks regain their health, but some of them even wound up leading far more robust lives than they had ever dreamed possible.

In spite of all the information available, most Americans continue to neglect their need for a consistent and full supply of the required nutritional elements. There are many reasons for this oversight. However, in my view, the greatest cause is that most people fail to transform their way of thinking about eating. They are only thinking about eating what they like and not which foods can assist their well-being. To improve your approach to eating, you must first learn of the three main elements that contribute to this problem. These three factors make up what I call the CIA factor, which stands for convenience, ignorance, and addiction.

Convenience: Detrimental to our nation's well-being, junk foods are obtainable virtually everywhere and continue to grow in popularity. To prove this point simply look at all the sugary, refined goodies which are available at our convenience stores: pastries, pies, cookies, cakes, and chips have practically taken over, and refrigerated sections of stores are loaded with sugary drinks and alcohol. In addition, fast-food restaurants are overwhelming our streets and boulevards, making healthy eating a rather challenging task. The reality is that food manufacturers and fast-food establishments are able to thrive simply by recognizing and utilizing the convenience factor to their advantage. Although this approach has helped increase their profits, it has also resulted in producing a society of consumers that is far less interested and informed about the importance of healthy eating. This frequently leads people to select the quickest, easiest and most unnutritious foods available. It is more life-enhancing if we avoid these foods and choose to prepare more of our own meals. This will help us evade the unwholesome convenience foods. Although this approach takes additional effort, it has the potential to bring tremendous health dividends.

Ignorance: Quite frankly most people do not know enough about nutrition to eat optimally. While they have some idea that vegetables are good for them, when was the last time you ate brown rice, whole wheat, or other whole grain cereals? In all likelihood, your answer is probably never or at best not very often for the simple reason that most people are not fully aware of the nutritional value of these foods. Alexander Schauss alludes to this problem in his book *Diet, Crime, and Delinquency,* where he states that, "In 1971, America had the distinction of becoming the first nation on earth to consume processed foods for more than 50 percent of it's diet." To reverse this trend, I recommend that you become more knowledgeable in this area by reading a minimum of three nutrition and health-oriented books. This step can assist you in developing a base of nutritional information and provide a guideline for healthful living.

Addiction: Practically everyone in our society is addicted to something—prescription drugs, illegal drugs, alcohol, caffeine, cigarettes, or even sugar. Nearly everyone has some sort of addiction which they feel compelled to satisfy. By ingesting the substance, an initial quick lift is provided but eventually the user is left feeling worse off than before he consumed the substance, which of course, simply makes the individual want to use even more of the addictive stimulant. What occurs with addicts is that the substances have taken over so effectively that they are no longer in charge of their lives. In my own case, I never would have believed that I was hooked on sugar. After all, I only ate dessert at night, how could I possibly be a sugar junkie? However, sugar is liberally added to most prepackaged foods which I ate in abundance. Whatever your fixation, it is essential that you take the requisite steps to regain control of your life. This might be difficult but it is necessary if you are truly serious about reaching your goals.

The CIA factors just discussed are three key issues that need to be addressed before you can ever even hope to improve your health. In order to enhance your well-being, you have to first become aware as to why you choose to eat the way you do. You will then become more capable of adhering to a health-building regimen.

Denatured Foods

The biggest problem with the so called "Standard American Diet" is its excessive reliance on processed foods. These foods which include sugar, white flour, refined grains, hydrogenated oils and fats, as well as most packaged foods, which have had many of their nutritional elements removed during processing procedures. Most of these nutrients are not added back during the enrichment process. For example, when whole wheat is processed to white flour over 22 known nutrients are removed, while only six are restored by enrichment.

The human body requires all of these elements for proper metabolic functioning. As a result of eating refined foods, many people develop nutritional deficiencies and corresponding illnesses. To avoid this scenario, we should eat foods in their complete, unrefined form. These whole foods are better able to assist us in attaining and maintaining harmony between our body, mind, and spirit.

In recent decades, we took a detour from nature and began to process more of our foods. A big turning point for the processed food industry came in 1943, when the Food and Drug Administration released this statement:

"Even though adequate nutrition could be better assured through the choice of natural foods than through reliance on enrichment, unenriched foods of the kinds and in the quantities necessary for adequate nutrition are now not available to substantial parts of the population and are not likely to be available soon; nor are most consumers sufficiently educated on nutritional questions to enable them to make an intelligent choice of combinations of unenriched foods on the basis of nutritional values. Because of the lack of adequate production of a number of foods high in certain nutrients and the lack of consumer knowledge of nutrition, appropriate enrichment of a few foods widely consumed by the population in general or by significant population groups will contribute substantially to the nutritional welfare of consumers and to meeting their expectations of benefit."

What was intended to be used as a temporary aid due to previous food supply shortages has inadvertently created a false belief among most consumers that enriched foods are equivalent to or better than whole, unrefined foods. This absurd notion has helped produce a nation of nutritional illiterates who believe that diet has little or no relation to health.

In contrast, many physicians, nutritionists, and health advocates, such as Doris Rapp, M.D., Adelle Davis, Carlton Fredricks, Ph.D., and Emanuel Cheraskin, M.D., have long claimed that many people are suffering with nutritional deficiencies and would benefit greatly by following a diet high in unrefined foods. Their reasoning is that whole foods provide a reliable supply of nutrients, fiber, and enzymes which allow every cell of the body to receive sufficient levels of the essential elements required for optimum metabolic functioning. A diet of whole foods will then enable our bodies' natural detoxifiction system to work more effectively and eliminate toxic chemicals, heavy metals, or poisons to which we are exposed. We will be better able to prevent and even recover from some of the more persistent health problems like obesity, diabetes, hypoglycemia, digestive disorders, heart disease, cancer, senility, and even some forms of mental illness. It is thus strongly recommended that we follow a diet which largely consists of whole, natural foods. In that way, we can positively affect our health, enabling us to achieve and preserve long lasting vibrant health.

Essential Fatty Acids

With all the negative press that fat has received one begins to wonder if it is even necessary for human health. However, as the phrase states, "essential fatty acids" are indeed mandatory. The reason that their presence is needed is simply because the human body cannot produce the three essential fats (arachidonic, linoleic, and linolenic) also known as vitamin F. These fats are needed to help maintain optimum functioning of each cell membrane and for the nerve sheath which protects and aids the performance of our nerves. It is also required for the formation and proper balance of prostaglandins, which are regulator substances produced and used by all cells of the body. Furthermore, vitamins A, D, E, and K cannot be properly utilized without a certain amount of fat. Needless to say, without receiving a sufficient amount of fat our body would be unable to operate properly, inevitably leading to serious health problems. It is essential that we provide ourselves with the fat we need to function effectively.

Before we can do this, it is necessary to become educated about the different types of fat and which ones promote health and which fats contribute to illness. Currently many people have the mistaken assumption that all vegetable oils or polyunsaturated vegetable oils are superior to saturated animal fats like butter, especially in regard to lowering cholesterol levels. However, quality nutritionists and health experts strongly disagree with this view citing that these partially hydrogenated oils are far less desirable. One reason that this false belief was perpetuated is that food processors saw an opportunity to increase profits, as well as the shelf life of oils, by pushing hydrogenated vegetable fats. A campaign was then initiated to educate America about the alleged benefits of these refined oils. At the time we were not aware that the modified vegetable fats and oils such as margarine, vegetable shortening, and most commercial (partially hydrogenated) vegetable oils, were so detrimental to health. The potential for harm exists because commercial oils are hydrogenated and heated to very high temperatures, up to 1000 degrees Fahrenheit. These high temperatures cause an alteration in the molecule, changing the fatty acid from its natural form to a unnatural trans fatty acid.

Additionally, when fats are refined, nutrients crucial to maintaining healthy cholesterol levels are also removed. Vitamins E, pyridoxine(B6), and the minerals chromium, and magnesium are not only subtracted during refinement but are not replaced by enrichment. Despite these nutritional losses, trans fats continue to be used abundantly in many commercial processed foods, such as salad dressing, crackers, cookies, pastries, cakes, dougnuts, french fries, chips, and fried chicken. According to Sherry A. Rogers M.D., the problem is that trans fatty acids do not fit into the lipid of cell membranes as effectively as the natural cis (non-hydrogenated) fats. Furthermore, the delta-6-desaturase enzymes which help metabolize good essential fatty acids into the membranes for peak performance are inhibited when trans fats are consumed. Thus, our cells are unable to get the quality fat they need to function optimally. These altered fats have been linked as contributors to some very unpleasant ailments like cancer, skin conditions, as well as cardiovascular and gastrointestinal disorders. With all that is currently known about the harmful effects of trans fatty acids, it is very questionable as to whether the hydrogenation process should even be continued.

It is important to note that beneficial fats which are found in cold pressed oils have a drawback also. These oils tend to spoil more rapidly than do trans fats. This spoilage occurs when oil is exposed to heat in the presence of oxygen. Therefore, if you are switching from trans fats to cold pressed oils, it is suggested that you refrigerate oils, with the exception of olive, immediately after they are purchased. It is also usually recommended that you keep oil for no more than 6 months; beyond this time the oil can become rancid.

The two main types of non-hydrogenated, polyunsaturated fatty acids which we need are omega 3 and omega 6 fats. Omega 3 fats or EPA (eicosapentaenoic acid) are predominantly found in cold water fish like tuna, salmon, trout, and halibut. However, walnuts, pumpkin and especially flax seeds are also excellent sources of EPA.

The omega 6 fats or GLA (gamma linoleic acid) are found primarily in seeds and nuts of warm weather plants such as safflower, sunflower, sesame, corn, and almond. Supplements of evening primrose oil, black currant and borage oil are high in already formed GLA and are therefore more easily utilized.

I like to supplement with a combination of both flax and borage oils to make certain that my body is getting its required level of both omega 3 and omega 6 fats. A good range for oil is probably 1-2 tablespoons daily. However, since everyone is different, you will need to consult with a health care professional.

It is strongly suggested that you take the necessary steps to avoid trans fats and instead choose to eat the healthy, cold-pressed oils. For cooking and meal preparation, I recommend that you use stable cold-pressed oils like olive, sesame, safflower, and corn oil, as they are generally regarded as more healthful. You should also reduce your consumption of saturated fat like beef and pork and replace it with lean protein sources like fish, legumes, chicken, turkey, and unrefined nuts and seeds. In this way you will supply your body with the beneficial fats needed for optimum functioning, while at the same time cut down on the damaging fats. Interestingly, in spite of all the negative attention that butter has received, it is actually significantly less detrimental to health than is the trans fatty acid-containing margarine. In fact, some may temporarily need saturated animal fats to help heal certain conditions of ill health. Check with your nutritionally-oriented physician or nutritional consultant to determine what approach will be best for your situation.

The Health Reducers

This section is dedicated to the body and/or mind altering substances which when abused, have a harmful effect over your health and quality of life. These substances, which include refined sugar, alcohol, cigarettes, caffeine, fluoridated water, synthetic food additives, prescription drugs, and illegal drugs, have several common ties when misused. All of the health reducers have the ability to contribute to the deterioration of health and premature aging, can worsen current conditions of inflammation in the body and deplete or interfere with the absorption of nutrients. Plus, other than fluoridated water, some food additives and certain medications all are potentially addictive. It is thus suggested that you either avoid, reduce, or utilize the above substances only when warranted.

Sugar

Probably the most commonly refined substance that is mass consumed today is sugar (sucrose). This is true for two major reasons. First, sugar has addictive powers that leave those who eat it longing for more; and second is that refined sugar is used abundantly in most processed foods. As a result, consumption of refined sugar is now at an all-time high.

The problem is that sugar is a nutritionally inferior food, which when eaten excessively can contribute to a whole host of health problems. Included in this list of potential ailments and problems are cardiovascular disturbances, cancer, diabetes, obesity, acne, hypoglycemia, ADD and hyperactivity, dental diseases, a weakened immune system, auto-immune disorders, yeast infections, nutritional deficiencies, inflammatory problems, premature aging, and an inability to think clearly. In view of this extensive list of perils, it is important that we learn to reduce our consumption of this health-reducing substance.

To achieve this objective, not only should you eat smaller dessert portions, but you should also learn to select processed foods which add little or no refined sugar. This means cutting down on most commercial-brand processed foods. Included in this list of sugar-laden foods are most commercial brands of jam or jellies, bread, beer, most wines, catsup, sauces, spreads, salad dressings, canned goods, breakfast cereals, soft drinks, and fruit juices. In fact, some 8 ounce bottles of soda contain as much as 7 teaspoons of sugar and many of the popular breakfast cereals have a sugar content as high as 40 percent, making it the cereal's main ingredient. Due to this sugar barrage, health advocates Gary and Steven Null claim that the average American now eats 31 to 50 teaspoons of sugar daily. In their book, *Orthomolecular Nutrition*, Abram Hoffer M.D., and Morton Walker D.P.M., also mention sugar's increased consumption as a concern, claiming that over the past three centuries, its use has increased from five pounds per person to about one hundred twenty-five pounds per person per year. While its elevated use is due mostly to the increased availability of sugar, do not forget about sugar's potent ability to attract users.

Refined sugar has powerful addictive qualities, even causing withdrawal symptoms for the junkie when it is removed from his diet. According to Annemarie Colbin, author of *Food and Healing*, "Getting off sugar is akin to getting off an addictive drug. People get cravings and headaches, feel depressed, fatigued, and are generally dispirited." Author William Dufty, concurred with this point in his book, *Sugar Blues*, claiming that he went through very unpleasant symptoms when eliminating it from his diet. The good news, however, is that once one gets it out of one's system one feels like a new person. Several people I met earlier in the HEAL of Central New York support group had initially experienced indications of withdrawal, but later felt great improvement and revival. It is therefore best that we strive to limit our consumption of this potent and alluring substance by at least 50 percent. Doing so will likely leave us with greater mental alertness, an enhanced sense of well-being, as well as a stronger immune system. This step will enable people to experience a higher quality of life than those who continue to overuse this excessively processed food. Eating less sugar can be one of the best self-investments that you can possibly make. To learn more about avoiding the hidden sugars in your food, read the Optimum Eating section of this chapter.

Cigarettes

Other than illegal drugs, smoking may be the most self-damaging activity in which you can engage. Largely due to its ability to contribute to the development of lung cancer and emphysema. However, in addition to these horrible ailments, smoking can also deplete the body of nutrients like Vitamins C and E, likely leading to deficiency diseases. This situation puts the individual in a vulnerable position and creates an internal environment which encourages a number of potential problems like heart attacks, cancer, weakened immunity, dental disease, accelerated aging, and severely deprives the entire body of oxygen.

A 1993 study proved smoking's devastating health effects. Medical literature from 1977-1993 was reviewed to determine the main causes of premature death in America. Tobacco products were cited as the number-one killer of Americans, with poor diet and a lack of exercise being a close second. Besides these factors, cigarette smoke is not only hazardous to the smoker but can also adversely impact those who are nearby. If small children or sick individuals are within our environment, it is even more important that we not smoke so that they can breathe fresh air.

With all of its destructiveness, one wonders why anyone in their right mind would continue to smoke? The answer is simply because smoking is an extremely addictive activity that becomes progressively more difficult to stop. In my view, the best way to address this problem and achieve cessation, is to use an approach that incorporates a good balance of proper nutrition, exercise, and counseling. The SmokEnders program by Jacquelyn Rogers which is thoroughly explained in her book, *You Can Stop Smoking*, fits the bill. If you currently smoke, I suggest that you get a copy and begin working to eliminate this nasty habit.

Note that smokers on average make four concerted efforts to stop before achieving non-smoker status. Do not get discouraged if you are initially unsuccessful. Just learn from each experience and keep trying until victorious.

Alcohol Abuse

Despite the many problems associated with alcoholism, abuse of this drug continues to be widespread. This is bad news, because long-term over-indulgence of alcohol can lead to a host of problems like liver damage, protein deficiency, anemia, early aging, nutritional deficiencies, and increased blood fat levels. Interestingly, according to nutritional authors Eleanor Noss Whitney and Eva May Nunnelley Hamilton, the negative effects of alcohol (ethanol) can be seen in the liver even after one night of binge drinking. The weakened liver then interferes with the allotment of nutrients and oxygen to the liver cells.

Besides hindering the absorption of nutrients, ethanol can also cause the kidneys to excrete increased quantities of nutrients such as magnesium, zinc, calcium, and potassium, further adding to health difficulties. Nutritional deficiencies thus become a major concern for the individual with a drinking problem.

For those who are seeking help, Alcoholics Anonymous or other support groups provide some of the guidance needed to deal with this addiction. Likewise, assistance from a nutritionist may also be crucial, because it is frequently necessary to correct nutritional deficiencies. Not surprisingly, alcohol treatment centers like the Health Recovery Center in Minneapolis, which employs nutrition and dietary improvements, have shown some of the most effective long-term results. Therefore, it is recommended that dietary improvements be part of every alcohol recovery program.

Warning: Alcohol is a substance that if consumed must be used with great caution. If you choose to drink alcoholic beverages, they should only be consumed by healthy people without substance abuse problems on occasion and in moderation.

Caffeine

With the exception of sugar, caffeine is likely one of the most frequently overlooked health weakeners. It is a substance obtained in coffee, teas, colas, some soft drinks, or in certain products for energy and pain relief. However, some nutritional health educators claim that it has some harmful effects, especially when consumed excessively. For example, Dr. Jeffrey Bland, in his book, *Your Health Under Siege*, states that, "Caffeine prolongs the action of adrenaline, which is known to be a hormone stimulating substance. Thus, it acts as a stimulant to the cardiac muscle, to the central nervous system, and to the secretion of gastric acid (which accounts for the frequency of ulcers in individuals who drink a lot of coffee)." He further added that excessive caffeine consumption contributes to elevated blood fat levels, and possibly even increases the potential for pregnant women to bear children with birth defects. For this reason, it is probably best that pregnant women abstain or at least dramatically reduce their consumption of caffeine during pregnancy and breast feeding.

Author Gary Null claims that excessive caffeine use can weaken the immune system making one vulnerable to disease. This is likely due to its ability to interfere with the absorption of calcium, as caffeine products increase our need for urination.

All of these factors, plus its addictive effects, make caffeine a powerful substance which if consumed excessively could impede your quest for a vibrant existence. It is probably best that we use caffeine products only in moderation and instead drink decaffeinated coffees and teas. Rather than using caffeine as an energy stimulant, we should eat properly, get sufficient rest, and exercise regularly. Consistently done, this will provide you with all the energy needed to take on the day and pursue your wellness goals.

Artificial Food Additives

According to the processed food industry, artificial food additives are harmless when consumed in small quantities. While this may be true, the unfortunate reality is that the average American eats a tremendous amount of processed food, which typically contains a number of different food additives. The cumulative amount of preservatives which we eat is actually quite significant, possibly making our exposure to these substances harmful. Food processors have also claimed that these additives are safe because the FDA has approved use of certain additives as safe or GRAS (generally recognized as safe). The evidence unfortunately does not fully prove their claims; in fact, some food additives appear to be linked to health problems. Monosodium glutamate, for example, has long been associated with allergic reactions, while the now banned red dye #2 was cited as a possible contributor to cancer. Some food additives may be fine when taken alone, but when eaten in combination with others could form a chemical reaction that makes them toxic. As a result, an unnecessary strain may be placed on the body's natural detoxification system. Thus, their intake is best kept to a minimum.

The elderly and sick, as well as young children, are more likely to be negatively affected by synthetic food additives, because their bodies are already working overtime to repair, sustain and grow. Food additives just give their overworked bodies one more unnecessary substance to detoxify and eliminate.

Reducing additive-laden foods would be wise for us all, for the simple reason that we do not know the cumulative effects they will have on our health. To achieve this goal, it is best that we structure our diet around unrefined foods.

Misusing Prescription Drugs

When properly used, prescription drugs are a very useful tool for combating many types of ailments and afflictions. I am also convinced that in many cases they are frequently misused. This can usually be best seen in people who have saved up a stockpile of medicine from previous doctor visits. These medicines are then used to serve as their own personal pharmacy, which they utilize at the slightest sign of a symptom. Besides the obvious danger that the novice may misdiagnose his symptoms and take something which could be inappropriate for his situation, he or she could also be masking the warning signal of pain. We must understand that aches, pains, and other symptoms are actually **warnings**, which our body sends to inform us that we are not functioning optimally. If we are consistently shutting off the pain without determining its cause, we may actually further increase the strain on our already ailing body. Then, over the next several years, the problem grows progressively worse until a more severe warning signal appears.

To avoid this type of predicament, we need to listen to our bodies and take on a larger role in matters relating to our health. This should start with seeking the advice of both our physician and nutritional consultant. They can assist you in determining the underlying causes of any symptoms, as well as devising a comprehensive plan to help address your situation. Then it will be your responsibility to make the positive lifestyle changes that are recommended. Certainly, this type of thorough approach will be much more effective at improving your situation rather than just masking your symptoms with medication.

Prescription drugs, when used properly, are an essential part of good health care. However, just like anything, medicine can be abused and should only be used when deemed necessary by your physician.

Overuse of Antibiotics

By helping our body to fight and destroy certain bacterial infections, antibiotics have made and will continue to make our nation a healthier place. Unfortunately though, abuse and misuse of these medicines can also have a very disturbing effect on our immune system. This typically occurs when patients who are experiencing a minor cold or virus pressure their doctor to prescribe and eventually get an antibiotic even when their physician says that it is not necessary. As far back as 1969, Curtis Baylor, M.D., stated in his book, *Common Sense Medicine,*

"There is evidence today that leads many immunologists to believe that indiscriminate use of antibiotics interferes with the normal development of protective immunity against the particular bacteria causing the sickness. In other words, for uncomplicated colds, grippe, mild influenza, simple diarrhea, or an occasional boil, it is wiser to rely on one's own immunity and simple medication than to use antibiotics." So even thirty-one years ago, it was known that antibiotics were to be used only when necessary. However, all too often patients continue to demand that their physician prescribe antibiotics even after they have been deemed unnecessary.

This is important to restate because if antibiotics are overused they can dramatically alter the intestinal environment by reducing or eliminating the beneficial intestinal microorganisms and by contributing to the growth of harmful microbes. This then sets the stage for all types of health problems like chronic infections, gastrointestinal irritation, antibiotic intolerance, or leaky gut syndrome. Because of these difficulties, some physicians now recommend that after their patients have taken antibiotics that they be followed with acidolphilus supplementation. The reason for this is that acidolphilus supplements contain healthy microorganisms, which help to restore the beneficial intestinal flora back to proper balance.

However, in certain instances when antibiotics are not necessary, many nutritionally oriented physicians are now recommending certain natural healing supplements. This list includes such substances as bovine colostrum, vitamin C, olive leaf extract, oil of oregano, garlic, royal jelly, bee propolis, and bee pollen. All of these natural infection fighters have strong healing benefits and are typically free of the harsh side effects associated with most prescription drugs.

Nonetheless, I want to be very clear that, when used appropriately, antibiotics are a wonderful tool which doctors use to effectively treat their patients. However, when misused, problems like antibiotic resistance or yeast overgrowths can arise. Therefore, it is important that we leave the decision of whether these drugs are necessary to our physician. In this way, we can hopefully prevent the majority of cases of misuse and maintain a proper level of beneficial microorganisms in our gastrointestinal tract necessary for good health.

Illegal Substances

Illegal substances include such mind-altering drugs as heroin, cocaine, LSD, and marijuana. These and other drugs wreck havoc in our society by damaging the lives of both its users and their families.

They do this initially by preventing people from gaining control of their lives, effectively stopping them from ever reaching their true potential. Then, when the problem becomes severe, addicts are frequently forced to choose between satisfying their addiction or fulfilling the needs of their careers and loved ones. Thus, before you or someone you love has deteriorated to a severe stage of addiction, it is advised that they seek aid in overcoming their addiction. In so doing, they can achieve a significant amount of personal growth, which is in my opinion necessary to overcoming any addiction.

As you might expect, dietary and lifestyle improvements are also typically helpful in breaking the grip of these substances. Simply going cold turkey without a thorough plan of attack usually leads to broken promises and a return to drug usage. Rather than this route, get involved in a recovery program which utilizes nutrition. This is typically necessary for two reasons. First, drugs tend to interfere with the absorption of nutrients, leaving the user malnourished. Second, addicts tend to eat very poorly, further contributing to the development of nutritional deficiencies. If left unresolved, these deficiencies could forever leave the individual craving the addictive substance. It is therefore necessary that addicted individuals employ a more comprehensive approach to help address their chemical dependencies. This should also supply them with the required energy necessary to return back to a sober, healthy state.

Fluoridated Water

Although many believe that fluoridated water is helpful in impeding tooth decay, much of the current evidence does not support this claim. For example, in the November 1995 issue of the *Townsend Letter for Doctors and Patients*, Richard Foulkes, M. D., states that "fluoridation does not prevent tooth decay, but (rather) it contributes to dental fluorosis (brown spots on teeth) and other adverse health effects."

The adding of fluoride to water started shortly after the fluoridation experiment which started on January 25, 1945, as reported by John Yiamouyiannis in *Fluoridation: The Aging Factor*. In his publication, he writes that the state of Michigan initially introduced fluoridated water to the public in Grand Rapids, with nearby Muskegon used as the non-fluoridated control group. These two cities, which were observed over a five-year period, saw cavity rates fall at about the same pace. Yet, for some strange reason, the U.S. Public Health Service discontinued the survey in Muskegon and only reported that cavities had decreased in Grand Rapids, after fluoridation. By not reporting that Muskegon had also experienced similar results, the U.S. Public Health Service failed to inform the public fully of the known facts. Amazingly, this misleading information continues to be used as a reason for adding fluoride to our water supply.

Other recent reports indicate that drinking fluoridated water increases risks of hip and neck fractures. According to the May 25, 1991, issue of *Science News*, women over 55 who consume highly fluoridated water for 20 or more years are more prone to fractures than women in non-fluoridated areas. Likewise, another study at the University of Utah found that men 65 and older, who were exposed to 20 plus years of fluoridated water had a 40 percent increased risk of hip fractures.

The 1983 *Physicians Desk Reference* also weighed in on this issue stating that,

"in hypersensitive individuals, fluorides occasionally cause skin eruptions, such as atopic dermatitis, eczema or urticaria. Gastric distress, headache and weakness have also been reported. These reactions usually disappear promptly after discontinuation of the fluoride." This advice was also reiterated by Michael Elsohn, D.D.S., who claims that some people may react adversely to fluoride contained in pills, water or toothpaste.

While some recommend the use of distilled water, it is my view that pure spring water from non-polluted sources is probably your best bet. At the very least use some type of filtration system to reduce the amount and concentration of pollutants like lead which may be present in our water supply. Whether you choose spring, distilled, or filtered, all are in my judgment vastly superior to unfiltered tap water.

In review, the health reducers are foods and/or substances that are best either eliminated, consumed less frequently, or used only when recommended by your physician. In this way, you will lower your exposure to these health-weakening substances, enabling you to live a more vigorous and hearty life, which is of course the ultimate goal that we are striving to achieve.

Diet & Supplements

Today nutritional supplements are used by approximately 40 percent of Americans who are concerned that they are not getting all of their nutritional requirements from their diet. To help combat nutritional deficits, the Food and Drug Administration has set guidelines the RDA, (recommended dietary allowances) that they consider to be safe and effective in supplementing the diet of the so-called average healthy individual. However according to many health advocates, people who are under any type of stress require higher levels of nutrients. Stress factors can include illness or disease, a fast-paced lifestyle, crisis situations, pressure on the job or at school, harmful relationships, and exposure to chemicals or toxic matter. Although it is recommended that we try to avoid these tense situations, it is virtually impossible to eliminate them altogether. Thus, we must learn how to handle the stress which is associated with these type of situations. In addition to stress reduction techniques like meditation, it is also necessary that we supply our body with a sufficient cross-section of nutrients. If our nutritional needs are not met through diet and food supplements, then our body will be unable to function at its highest level, which will likely leave us in a weakened state and more vulnerable to illness. However, if our nutritional requirements are met then we will be much more able to handle stress effectively and preserve our wellness.

The following chart is designed to expand your awareness of which nutrients are contained in our foods, their functions, signs of deficiency, and the recommended daily allowances. It should be used to help you plan meals around nutritious, health enhancing foods.

Nutrients	Sources	Functions	Deficiency Signs	RDA
Vitamin A	orange and yellow veggies and fruits, greens, eggs, liver, bee pollen, fish & flax oils.	Prevents premature aging, builds resistance, good for eye function, promotes vitality.	Poor vision, skin disorders, less resistance to infections, lack of appetite.	5000 IU
Vitamin B-1 (Thiamine)	whole grains, seeds, nuts, beans, dairy, liver, greens, and bee pollen.	Promotes growth, prevents fatigue, preserves health of nervous system.	Loss of weight, wasting of tissues, beriberi, depression, fatigue.	1.5 mg
Vitamin B-2 (Riboflavin)	whole grains, liver, brewer's yeast, dairy, bee pollen.	For growth and health of eyes, growth.	Anemia, ulcers, vaginal itching,	1.7 mg
Vitamin B-3 (Niacin)	Brewer's yeast, whole grains, liver, seafood, seeds, nuts, and bee pollen.	Maintains G.I. function, promotes healthy circulation, and skin.	Headaches, depression, digestive disorders, pellagra, mental illness.	20 mg
Vitamin B-5 (Pantothenic Acid)	Brewer's yeast, whole grains, legumes, liver, green veggies, eggs, bee pollen.	Stimulates adrenal glands, anti-stress vitamin, can help prevent premature aging.	Fatigue, infections, stomach problems, hypoglycemia, skin disorders.	10 mg
Vitamin B-6 (Pyridoxine)	Brewer's yeast, liver, whole grains, soybeans, eggs, dairy, nuts, carrots, cabbage, molasses, and bee pollen.	Prevents tooth decay, dream recall, essential for nervous system and brain, monitors balance between minerals in the body.	Carpal tunnel syndrome, PMS, anemia, colitis, tooth decay, headaches and halitosis.	2 mg
Folic Acid (folate)	Greens, brewer's yeast, liver, nuts, legumes, bee pollen, and whole grains.	Essential for formation of red blood cells, healthy skin and hair.	Anemia, fatigue, skin disorders, fatigue & depression	400 mcg
Biotin	Brewer's yeast, whole grains, liver, soybeans, healthy intestinal	Necessary for healthy hair, prevents hair loss, antiseptic qualities.	Eczema, dandruff, hair loss, fatigue and depression	.3 mg

bacteria, bee pollen.

Nutrients	Sources	Functions	Deficiency Signs	RDA
PABA Para-Amino Benzoic Acid	Brewer's yeast, whole grains, eggs, liver, dairy, and bee pollen.	Stimulates metabolism, prevents graying hair, soothes sunburns, essential for healthy skin.	Fatigue, anemia, gray hair, reproductive disorders.	--
Choline	Soybeans, liver, lecithin, eggs, brewer's yeast, greens, dairy, legumes and bee pollen.	Reducing high blood pressure, prevents glaucoma, regulates liver and gall bladder.	High blood pressure, degeneration of the arteries.	--
Vitamin B-12 (Cobalamin)	Liver, dairy, kelp, kombu, wakame, nuts, seeds, eggs, meats, bananas, and bee pollen.	Essential for production and regeneration of red blood cells, promotes growth in children	Chronic fatigue, premature aging, thyroid problems, difficulty in concentrating.	6.0 mcg
Vitamin C (Ascorbic Acid)	Raw fruits and vegetables, fruits, greens, bee pollen	Essential for production of healthy collagen functions of the organs, natural antibiotic.	Tooth decay, premature aging, lowered resistance, scurvy	60 mg
Vitamin P (Bioflavonoids)	Fresh fruits and vegetables, citrus fruits.	Protects vitamin C in the body, strengthens capillary walls.	Varicose veins, bleeding gums, eczema.	--
Vitamin D	Fish liver oil, egg yolks sunlight, sunflower seeds, and bee pollen.	Assimilation of calcium essential for healthy thyroid, promotes strong teeth and bones.	Tooth decay, osteoporosis, retards growth, rickets.	400 IU
Vitamin E (Alpha-Tocopherol)	Unrefined vegetable oils, seeds, nuts, eggs, greens, whole grains and bee pollen.	Oxygenates the tissues, retards aging, essential for healthy reproductive organs.	Reproductive disorders, anemia, varicose veins, miscarriage.	30 IU
Vitamin K	Leafy greens, kelp liver, acidophilus and bee pollen	Aids liver function, anti- hemorrhaging vitamin, increases vitality.	Nosebleeds, ulcers, premature aging, lowered vitality	40 mcg
Vitamin F (Essential Fatty Acids)	Vegetable oils such as; flax, sesame, corn, borage & evening primrose	Lowers blood cholesterol essential for adrenal glands, can protect from radiation damage.	Skin disorders, falling hair, prostate disorders, PMS	--

oil.

Minerals	Sources	Functions	Deficiency Signs	RDA
Calcium (Ca)	Greens, complex minerals, dairy, whole grains, sesame seeds, and bee pollen	Builds healthy teeth and bones, essential for heart action and muscle activity.	Osteoporosis, tooth decay, depression, heart palpitations, spasms, insomnia, irritability.	1000-1500 mg
Phosphorus (P)	Whole grains, seeds, nuts, eggs, dairy, shellfish, and bee pollen.	Works with calcium, important in mental activity, needed for enzyme function.	Retarded growth, reduced sexual power, general weakness.	1000 mg
Magnesium (Mg)	Soybeans, nuts, greens, whole grains, dairy, complex minerals, legumes, and bee pollen.	Detoxification, needed for healthy muscle tone, essential for healthy heart, regulates acid-alkaline balance	Toxemia, heart attack, premature wrinkles, epilepsy, kidney damage, muscle cramps, fatigue	400 mg
Potassium (K)	All vegetables, seeds, bananas, complex minerals, legumes, fruits, and bee pollen.	An alkalizing agent, essential for muscle contraction, detox.	Fatigue, high blood pressure, heart attack, constipation, nervous disorders.	775-5625 mg
Sodium (Na)	Sea salt, salt, tamari, meat, dairy, seafood root veggies, and bee pollen.	For production of acid in stomach, needed to maintain proper electrolyte balance.	Fatigue, depression, muscular weakness, heat exhaustion, diarrhea.	450-3300 mg
Chlorine (Cl)	Complex minerals, oats, veggies, especially celery, and bee pollen.	Essential for production of hydrochloric acid needed to help liver.	Poor digestion.	700 mg
Iron (Fe)	Liver, greens, nuts, legumes, meats, dairy, whole grains, and bee pollen.	Essential for formation of hemoglobin, builds up quality of the blood, increases resistance.	Anemia, pale complexion, low interest in sex, run down feeling.	10-18 mg
Copper (Cu)	Seafood, liver nuts, fruit, seeds, whole grains, mushrooms, and bee pollen.	Needed for production of RNA. Prevents anemia.	Anemia, loss of hair, digestive disturbances, heart problems.	2 mg

Minerals	Sources	Function	Deficiency Signs	RDA
Iodine (I)	Complex minerals, sea salt, seafood, egg yolks, fish liver oils, and bee pollen.	Essential for healthy thyroid, prevents rough wrinkled skin.	Goiter, loss of interest in sex.	150 mcg
Manganese (Mn)	greens, nuts, whole grains, fruit, veggies, complex minerals, eggs, and bee pollen.	Detoxification, needed for proper reproductive function, needed for function of mammary glands.	Digestive disturbances, retarded growth, sterility, asthma	1.5-5 mg
Zinc (Zn)	Oysters, legumes, meat, seafood, complex minerals, dairy, whole grains and bee pollen.	Needed for insulin molecules, needed by sex organs, aids immune system.	Loss of sense of taste and smell, birth defects, slow healing, hair and skin problems, prostate problems.	15 mg
Fluorine (F)	Whole grains, seeds, nuts, dairy, veggies, complex minerals.	Needed for healthy teeth and bones, protects against infections.	Cavities, brittle bones.	1-4 mg
Chromium (Cr)	Whole grains, liver, veggies, brewer's yeast, mushrooms.	Essential for utilization of sugar, works with insulin.	Diabetes, hypoglycemia, heart disease.	0.2mg
Molybdenum (Mo)	Legumes, greens, whole grains, liver, complex minerals, brewer's yeast, and bee pollen.	Detoxification, needed for proper carbohydrate metabolism, prevents copper poisoning.	Toxemia, hypoglycemia.	0.5mg
Selenium (Se)	Brewer's yeast, seafood, veggies, complex minerals, eggs, dairy, grains.	Works in combination with Vit. E, antioxidant, protects body from toxic substances.	Liver damage, premature aging, muscular atrophy, can lead to cancer.	0.2 mg
Silicon (Si)	Greens, seeds, whole grains, fruit, leafy greens, nuts, bee pollen.	Crucial for strong bones, teeth, hair, nails. Helpful in all healing processes.	Premature aging, insomnia, osteoporosis, skin disorders.	--

Nutrients	Sources	Function	Deficiency Signs	RDA
Trace Minerals	Dark leafy greens, complex ionic minerals, bee pollen.	Unknown.	Unknown.	--
Amino Acids	Leafy greens, soybeans, nuts, meats, dairy, seafood, liver, whole grains, seeds, bee pollen.	Building blocks of protein, needed for life, muscle builders, aids brain function.	Toxemia, anemia, allergies, etc	--
Dietary Fiber	Whole grains, fresh fruit and vegetables.	Cleans and maintains healthy digestive system.	Toxemia, digestive disorders.	--
Enzymes	Fermented foods such as: miso and tamari, raw fruit and vegetables, honey, and bee pollen.	For vitality, aids in digestion, speeds healing, increases vitality.	Fatigue, poor overall health, indigestion.	--

As you can see certain foods like dark leafy greens, colorful vegetables, whole grains, legumes, seeds, nuts, bee pollen, seafood, meats, poultry, dairy and fruit are nutritional powerhouses. If unprocessed versions of these foods comprise the majority of our diets, nutritional deficiencies and their corresponding symptoms will be very unlikely. These foods supply needed nutrients to our bodies in sufficient amounts so that we are able to function at a very high level. On the other hand, consuming mostly processed foods will eventually lead to deficits and contribute to conditions of ill health. This is why I am so high on eating these nutritious whole foods, for when I supply my body with what it requires, it responds by providing me with a high standard of life.

The key point to remember is that we cannot consistently eat processed foods and expect to build optimum health, simply because these foods no longer contain all the nutrients and fiber that are necessary for total health. An inferior diet will in all likelihood catch up with you and eventually reduce your overall quality of life. Many people cannot seem to understand this concept. They instead continue to eat the same denatured foods, over-consume soft drinks, coffee and alcohol, smoke cigarettes, then are amazed that their bodies do not operate effectively.

Even if eating properly and exercising regularly, other factors can contribute to nutritional deficiencies, like biochemical individuality. Many people, therefore, could benefit from an individualized and well-balanced, supplement program. Supplement plans which are properly prepared by nutritional consultants and nutritionally-oriented physicians, often produce great results. Abram Hoffer, Ph.D., M.D., and Humphrey Osmond, D.P.M., are excellent examples, who as leaders in the field of nutritional health, have done great work in this area. In addition to an effective diet, these men employ supplements to help correct their patient's nutritional shortages. Patients are then taught to sustain this balance through proper diet along with a modified supplement program.

Sadly though, most of our medical establishment has chosen largely to disregard nutritional approaches. The key reason for this was also discussed in the Sept/Oct 1993 issue of *Natural Health* magazine. In the article, "Dr.'s Fail Nutrition," it noted that of the 129 medical schools in the United States only 29 require nutritional course work. Thus, the individuals who graduate from these institutions are not fully prepared to educate the public on healing and health preservation.

Before I go on, I want to make it clear that despite its shortcomings, we still have the best medical system in the world. The treatments and continuing discoveries make our country the undisputed leader in medical technology. Likewise, our physicians are well-prepared to treat most of the problems they encounter, especially those of an acute nature. What I am saying is that our system could be better and more complete if nutrition and other natural healing methods were used in conjunction with orthodox medical treatments. It is therefore wise that we utilize a combination of the two approaches.

Christopher K. Sembera (BS, CNC, Be.P)

Nutritional Balance

As just stated, when used appropriately in conjunction with a proper diet, supplements can assist us in restoring and maintaining nutritional balance. This is important because as you saw from the nutrient charts, deficiencies can contribute to a whole host of difficulties.

To fully comprehend and access the benefits of supplementation, you must understand two things. First, that all nutrients are needed in ample amounts working harmoniously together. Only when we possess a full complement of nutrients can we effectively nourish our cells and rebuild our constantly changing existence.

The second point is that deficiencies rarely occur with just one nutritional element. If you are low in one nutrient, you will probably be lacking in others. Likewise, if your diet and supplement program does not contain a proper symmetry of all nutrients, you could be creating other nutritional imbalances. This is precisely why supplementing solely with one vitamin or mineral rarely works. An example of this could be the taking of only elementary iron supplements for anemia. The late nutritionist Adelle Davis stated emphatically that this could cause trouble because anemia has many causes such as shortages in vitamin E, B-6, folic acid, B-12, copper and magnesium, along with iron. Unless all of the underlying causes are discovered and addressed, the symptoms of imbalance associated with anemia can become more profound. In addition, some supplements like iron can become toxic and should only be used with great caution.

It is best that we try to solve our imbalances through diet and natural food products. However, if necessary, vitamin and mineral supplements will be recommended by your nutritional consultant to restore and preserve long-lasting nutritional equilibrium. Quick-fix approaches never truly resolve the situation and can sometimes create additional imbalances making the underlying condition worse.

While many health advocates recommend using a good daily multivitamin for health maintenance, I also like to eat or use natural food products like bee pollen, and green supplements such as yaeyama chlorella, barley and wheat grasses. These supplements are extremely nutritious and are generally easy to absorb. Since most of us find it difficult to eat organic whole foods regularly, these foods can provide the trace minerals in abundant amounts which our diets typically fail to do. These nutritious foods or their corresponding products should be a part of our daily rountine.

Allergic individuals generally find it necessary to use supplements which are free of sugar, starch, and dyes which are contained in some of the well-known brands. These additives can cause irritation and trigger allergic reactions for some individuals whose health is severely impaired. For further information, see the rear of this book for a listing of companies which sell hypo-allergenic nutritional supplements.

Should you desire additional reading on nutritional augmentation see, *The Right Dose*, by Patricia Hausman, M.S., *Earl Mindell's Vitamin Bible* by Earl Mindell, and *The Real Vitamin and Mineral Book* by Shari Lieberman and Nancy Bruning.

Disclaimer: *Always remember that there is no one supplement plan for everyone. Each plan needs to be prepared for each individual. Before starting any supplementation program you should seek the assistance of a nutritionist or nutritionally-oriented physician. He or she can design an individualized supplementation program especially suited to meet your body's needs.*

Nutritious Eating

American health care costs are climbing to unprecedented levels and show no signs of tapering off. If we are to improve this situation, our focus must be on creating an environment that fosters optimum health rather than just treating disease. To achieve this aim, proper diet must be emphasized as being one of the key ingredients for constructing a healthy nation.

A nutrititous eating approach is vital because the cells of the human body are in a continual process of deterioration and replenishment. If you have a health problem such as cancer, it is crucial that you understand that the cells you now possess will be replaced by entirely new cells in the upcoming weeks, months, and years. This is why it is essential that we properly nourish ourselves with the foods required for restoring and preserving optimum health. The plain, simple truth is that our future health status will in large part be determined by our current nutritional decisions. If we follow a wise eating plan today, we can actually prevent potential future cases of ill health and even, in some situations, reverse well-established instances of disease. In so doing, we will both enhance our quality of life and help to control our medical care costs.

To help you choose an effective health maintenance eating plan, it is suggested that you look for those that contain these four main components. A healthy eating approach should:

1. be high in unrefined foods;
2. be high in fiber;
3. limit consumption of the health reducers; and
4. emphasize balancing acid to alkaline foods and substances.

Unrefined Foods

As explained earlier, refined foods are inferior to unprocessed foods as they no longer contain all the vitamins and minerals which they had prior to processing. We also must not forget that so-called enriched products contain preservatives and additives, putting an additional strain on the body to eliminate these substances. The only proficient way to avoid these substances and supply our body with a constant supply of nutrients is to center our eating pattern around whole, natural foods. In so doing, we will provide our bodies with the raw materials necessary to achieve our ultimate level of wellness.

High-Fiber Foods

It is crucial that our diet be high in fiber. High-fiber foods are essential to a healthy human digestive system. In fact, information continues to mount recognizing the importance of dietary fiber in helping to maintain a sound gastrointestinal tract. Fiber is necessary to help cleanse and purify the long and winding intestinal tract which is approximately 24-27 feet in length.

Human dentition also appears more suited to a diet that is high in fiberous foods. We possess only 4 canine teeth which are most appropriate for tearing and cutting meat, while the other 28 teeth are perfectly suited for grinding whole grains, vegetables, nuts, seeds and fruit, all of which are high in fiber. It seems only logical that the majority of our dietary intake correlate with the way the human anatomy is composed.

- Before going on, I again want to make it clear that a significant percentage of people will react unfavorably to an eating method which is high in whole grains and other harsh fiber. Individuals who would be good candidates for this type of eating regimen would likely consist of those suffering with gastrointestinal disturbances, certain autoimmune and immune system disorders, or those who are trying to repair damage to their body after an injury or surgery. These people will, at least in the short term, typically need a dietary approach closer to Elaine Gottschall's, *Breaking the Vicious Cycle,* Dr Mercola's *Reaching for Optimum Wellness Diet* at mercola.com, or Dr. Sherry Rogers, transitional carnivore approach in her book, *Wellness Against All Odds.* These diets all stress the importance of getting adequate protein, fat, sea salt, vegetables, and vegetable juices while at the same time limiting or even temporarily eliminating grains from the diet. Grains for these people could, in the beginning, be a major irritant to their system. Another excellent approach that many people experience success with is documented by Dr. Peter D'Adamo in his national best selling book, *Eat Right for Your Blood Type.* To help determine which of these guidelines would better suit your needs, it is recommended that you see your physician and nutritional consultant.

Limit Consumption of the Health Reducers

As discussed previously, the health reducers interfere with the absorption of nutrients and are therefore either best eliminated altogether or at least eaten in moderation. If these foods and/or substances are consumed, it is advisable to make certain that our eating plan compensates sufficiently for the nutritional losses that

Christopher K. Sembera (BS, CNC, Be.P)

will be incurred when consuming the nutrient-depriving health reducers.

Acid/Alkaline Balance

Another reason that many health advocates recommend eating approaches which emphasize unprocessed foods is because these whole natural foods are rich in nutrients which help us maintain a balanced acid/alkaline blood level. This balance refers to the blood's pH balance of acid and alkaline, which is normally between 7.3 - 7.45.

To help maintain this balance, it is necessary that we do two things. First, we must consistently follow an eating plan which supplies a balanced cross-section of nutrients. In this way, the necessary nutrients will be provided to help stabilize and maintain a balanced acid/alkaline blood level.

Then, we need to limit our consumption of the strong acid-forming substances and foods. Otherwise nutrients, especially calcium and the B-vitamins, will be confiscated from our body to restore equilibrium of our acid/alkaline blood level. Continually repeated, this can cause a severe drain on our nutritional reserves and possibly lead to the development of nutritional deficiencies, chronic diseases, and premature aging.

In general, acid-forming foods include meats, legumes, nuts, and grains; whereas, alkaline forming foods are fruits, vegetables, sea vegetables, salt, and sea salt. Certain foods and substances like chemicals, drugs, tobacco products, overly refined foods, alcohol, and sugar are very acid-forming. While it would be ideal to avoid all of these foods or substances altogether, they should at least be significantly reduced. The interesting substance here is caffeine which has an alkalizing effect on the blood but increases acid production in the stomach. As a result, it is best consumed only in moderation. The following chart is designed to help illustrate these different groups.

Acid-Forming Foods	Alkaline-Forming Foods
Chemicals, drugs, tobacco, refined sugars, saccharin, vinegar, most food additives, meats, oils, most grains, nuts, beans. The nightshade vegetables like: tomatoes, potatoes, eggplant, and peppers are also acid forming.	*Caffeine, fruits, teas, most vegetables, seeds, sea salt, and salt.*

Milk, which is not mentioned above, is considered to be perfectly balanced between the two groups and will not have a significant impact either way on the acid/alkaline balance. It should be noted that raw and juiced foods tend to be more alkaline-forming, whereas cooked foods are typically more acidic. It is necessary that we eat a blend of both raw and cooked foods to help maintain a balance between the two.

By following these simple steps, we can maintain a healthy acid/alkaline balance which will help to preserve our body's nutritional reserves. Our chances of maintaining long-lasting health will be greatly enhanced.

For additional information on this matter, read Herman Aihara's book, Acid and Alkaline.

Optimum Eating
Whole Grains & Whole Grain Products

Macrobiotic educators like Michio Kushi, Herman Aihara, and the late George Oshawa have long said that whole grains and whole grain products should be the principal food for humans. They claim that this is wise because of their well-balanced, nutritional content which provides stable energy to those who regularly consume these foods. For centuries many early civilizations relied heavily on whole grains like wheat and barley as their staple food. Therefore, it is probably wise that we, too, consider making whole grains a key part of our daily diet.

It is of crucial importance that we first understand the differences between refined grains and whole grains. Adelle Davis in her book, *Let's Eat Right To Keep Fit,* uncovered figures provided by the Department of Agriculture which state that white bread, when compared to whole wheat bread, "has lost the following percents of nutrients: calcium, 60; potassium, 74; iron, 76; magnesium, 78; linoleic acid, 50; vitamin B-1, 90; Vitamin B-2, 61; and niacin, 80." She further listed other losses like: folic acid 79%, pyridoxine 60%, zinc 50%, pantothenic acid 69%, vitamin E 100%, manganese 84%, and copper 74%. You can rest assured that when other refined grains like white rice are compared to their unrefined counterpart (brown rice) similar shortages exist.

We must not forget that virtually all of the fiber has been removed and not replaced by enrichment. Remember that enrichment only replaces 6 of the 22 nutrients removed during processing. In addition, these starchy refined grains, after being eaten, are easily converted into sugar in the body. If this sugar is not used up by the body for energy then it becomes stored as fat. **The assertion that enriched white bread is nutritionally equivalent to whole wheat bread is simply not accurate.** Eating refined grains is an ineffective way of assisting your body in meeting its nutritional needs. Nonetheless, if you are in good health you may eat the so-called enriched grains occasionally.

BEST CHOICES: Consider consuming variety of whole grains including brown rice, millet, barley, ryeberries, wheatberries, oats, spelt, kamut, whole wheat couscous, quinoa, buckwheat, teff, and amaranth. Plus use whole grain breads and all products made strictly from 100% whole grain flours such as pastas, crackers, tortillas, pizza dough, pita bread, sugar-free breakfast cereals, etc.

Your second best bets include low-sugar breakfast cereals, popcorn, and all flour products which use a mix of both whole grains and refined grains.

Reduce consumption of white rice, corn, white flour, and all products made strictly from refined white flour, like pasta, cakes, rice cakes, sugary

Christopher K. Sembera (BS, CNC, Be.P)

breakfast cereals, breads, pastries, tortillas, pizza dough, cookies, and crackers.

* When buying flour products make certain that you read the label of ingredients to determine whether these are made from whole wheat or whole grain flours. What you want is to find products that list some type of whole grain flour as its first ingredient.

Fruits and Vegetables

Due to convenience, many people are now eating canned or frozen produce instead of fresh, locally grown fruit and vegetables. This, as we have discussed, creates two main problems. First is that the processing of these foods removes many nutritional benefits, and second is that the synthetic additives used in the processing of these foods are not helpful. Thus, it is best that we eat fresh fruits and vegetables whenever possible.

Vegetables: You need to eat a wide variety of this grouping, so that you will get a diverse supply of nutrients as well as fiber. Whenever possible, the skin should be left intact, for this is where most of the nutrients are located.

BEST CHOICES (Eat freely): dark leafy greens, broccoli, brussel sprouts, cabbage, summer squash, winter squash, cauliflower, carrots, bell peppers, lettuce, beets, string beans, snow peas, asparagas, artichokes, celery, parsnips, okra, fennel, cucumbers, tomatoes, sweet potatoes, onions, ginger, garlic, leeks, lemons, limes, daikon, rutabagas, turnips, radishes and mushrooms.

*Because they are easily converted into sugar, corn and potatoes are best eaten only in moderation. This includes corn and potato chips as well. ***However, sweet potatoes which contain more fiber are okay.***

*Avacados are rich in fat and should be eaten less frequently.

*Sprouts and prepacked lettuce mixes are more likely to contain preservatives, mold, and harmful bacteria and are therefore best avoided altogether.

*Canned or bottled vegetable juices are best used in moderation, as they no longer possess enzymes and typically contain additives or additional ingredients which are best avoided.

Raw Vegetable Juices (one pint of raw vegetable juice daily): Because of the tremendous source of nutrients like calcium, magnesium, potassium and enzymes that are contained in freshly prepared vegetable juices, juicing is very helpful in maintaining vibrant health. The research, work, and success stories documented by Jay "The Juiceman" Kordich, Norman Walker, D. Sc., and Max Gerson, fully support the consumption of these nutritious drinks. For more information on fresh vegetable juices, see chapter 16.

Due to their high nutritional content, everyone should consume at least two, 1 cup servings of dark leafy greens daily. Or else you can choose to drink fresh vegetable juices or one of the various green juice powders or pills like Greening Power or Bio-Green.

Fruit (2-4 servings): All types. A wide variety should be consumed, and try to eat those fruit that are locally grown as they will tend to be more fresh and delicious. Remember, it is best to leave the skin on fruit, as this is where many of the nutrients are located. When selecting fruit juices, jellies, and jams try to select those that are either unsweetened or contain only fruit juice concentrate.

*Frozen fruits and vegetables can be used; however, it is more desirable to eat fresh, locally grown, organic produce.

*Most dried fruits contain additives; select those from health food stores which are additive free.

Fiber

Fiber (five or more servings daily): As stated earlier, the daily consumption of fiber is crucial to the maintenance of a healthy digestive tract. Failure to satisfy your daily fiber requirements can, over a period of time, contribute to a number of health disturbances like constipation or even possibly colon cancer. You should consume at least your daily minimum of five high-fiber foods. High-fiber foods include whole grains, vegetables, fruit, seeds, nuts, and legumes.

Protein

Protein which consists of 22 amino acids is the building block of muscle. Yet it does much more, including helping to preserve, sustain, and build cells and tissues whenever the body deems it necessary. Eight of the amino acids are called essential, meaning that they must be supplied in our diets because the human body cannot manufacture them. Protein is thus a vital part of our diet which is necessary for proper metabolic functioning.

In spite of all the good that protein provides, excessive amounts can also potentially cause problems. In his book, *Eat To Win*, author and clinical nutritionist, Dr. Robert Haas, states that: "Protein metabolism releases toxic waste products (such as ammonia) which contributes to the final product of protein metabolism, urea, also a toxic substance. If you eat more protein than your body can use, your kidneys and liver must work harder to detoxify and remove these potential poisons. Since the body forms more urine to dispose of the increased ammonia and urea, vital minerals such as potassium, calcium, and magnesium are lost along with waste as your body dehydrates." To prevent this scenario, we need to keep an adequate balance of protein to whole grains, fruit and vegetables, and their juices.

* Although many people do well with a moderate intake of protein, amounts will vary and could be higher from person to person according to their metabolic body type, health status, and activity level. Consumption of protein should never be less than 12-15 percent of your daily intake.

Meat, Nuts, Legumes, Poultry, Fish, and Eggs (2-3 servings): Legumes, nuts, eggs, meats, poultry, fowl, wild game and seafood. Eat a wide variety of these foods to prevent boredom and to avoid falling into a rut with any one type of protein. This not only provides your body with a more thorough supply of nutrients but also can help prevent any food intolerances from developing.

BEST CHOICES *(Legumes):* All dry beans and peas are excellent. Tofu and tempeh, soybean products, are also good.

Remember though many people react to soy and soy-based products.

BEST CHOICES (*Seafood):* All. However, some people are allergic to shellfish. Avoid them if you fall into this category. Likewise, due to their mercury content, seafood is best eaten in moderation.

BEST CHOICES (*Meat and Poultry):* All. Yet, it is probably best to choose lean sources of meat and remove all skin and fat prior to cooking. Some health food stores carry naturally-raised meats, eggs and poultry, which can enable us to avoid the steroid and antibiotic remnants found in traditional animal products.

BEST CHOICES (*Nuts):* Unrefined, unroasted plain nuts like almonds, pecans, walnuts and chestnuts. Peanuts contain mycotoxins and are the least advantageous of the nuts. It is wise to limit our consumption of peanut butter as well. **Natural, sugar-free almond butter is an acceptable and delicious alternative**.

*Another nutrient not frequently mentioned, but that is helpful to brain function, is lecithin. It is found naturally in soy and egg yolks, so consider making these foods part of your dietary intake.

*Hot dogs, bacon, sausages, canned meats, and luncheon meats are usually loaded with food preservatives and are therefore best avoided or eaten in moderation.

Dairy/Dairy Substitutes

Although dairy products continue to be the most common source of calcium for most people, many people are lactose-intolerant and find that these foods cause them to experience gastrointestinal cramping and discomfort. While some of these folks find digestive enzyme products like Lactaid helpful, many others have discovered that consuming lactose-free dairy products solves their intolerance problems. Still others find dairy alternative foods like goat or soy milk to be their best option. Additional calcium-rich foods which should also be part of our diet are vegetable foods like legumes, dark leafy greens, raw vegetable juices, whole grains, and seeds and nuts. This is especially important to note because these foods are typically rich in other nutrients like magnesium which is needed to help properly absorb calcium. Thus, it is necessary that we eat a sufficient amount of these other foods. Remember though, that most dairy products, as well as some of their substitutes are high in fat. So our intake of these foods is usually best limited to the recommended 2-3 servings.

BEST CHOICES: Dairy/Dairy Substitutes (2-3 servings): plain skim and low-fat yogurt, skim and low-fat milk, various dairy cheeses, low-fat cottage cheese. Dairy substitutes include goat milk, goat cheese, soy milk, soy cheese, almond milk, and rice dream milk.

Dairy and dairy substitute foods that are rich in sugar or saturated fat include whole fat milk and yogurt, yogurt with fruit and sugar, butter, sour cream, cream cheese, cream, chocolate milk, ice cream and ice milk, frozen yogurt, and rice dream frozen treats. These foods are best eaten in moderation.

*Tiny fish with bones like sardines is yet another food source that is loaded with usuable calcium.

*Vitamin D is another nutrient which is required to absorb calcium, so make certain that you are getting enough in your diet.

*Remember that raw vegetables juices can also be used to help supply much needed calcium.

*For additional information on calcium and magnesium content in foods, see nutritional tables, for other foods rich in these nutrients.

*Condensed milk is so rich with sugar that it is best avoided altogether, or at least viewed as a sugar.

Christopher K. Sembera (BS, CNC, Be.P)

*Butter is saturated fat and is best consumed in moderation. Olive oil is a better choice.

Essential Fatty Acids

While it true that most Americans eat too much fat, another key problem is that the quality of fat consumed is of inferior value. In order to address this situation, it is recommended that you cut down on the saturated and trans fatty acids. This can be achieved by consuming reasonable portions of animal products and switching from hydrogenated fats to cold pressed oils. Seeds and nuts are also rich in essential fats and can help nourish the human body with beneficial fat.

BEST CHOICES: Essential Fat Oils (1 Tbs. daily): Olive, sesame, corn, and safflower in food preparation, with flax, borage, and evening primrose oil being used as supplemental fats.

Best uses of oils;
olive, safflower - sautéing, salad dressings, sauces
frying – safflower, peanut, corn
sesame – stir frying
corn, safflower – baking
flax, borage, evening primrose – (supplemental uses)

A total oil consumption of 1-2 tablespoons daily is probably a good range for many people. This total will include all oil that is used in cooking, salad dressings, supplementation, and in our seeds and nuts. However, individual needs will vary, so check with your doctor and nutritional consultant for determining your best level.

BEST CHOICES: Seeds (1-2 teaspoons per day): **Sesame (brown or black), flax, and pumpkin, are the preferred varieties.** Sunflower seeds are best eaten in moderation as they tend to turn rancid very rapidly because their protective shell is frequently removed prior to their sale. **Sesame butter or tahini which is high in calcium is also good.**

* Flax, borage, and evening primrose oil cannot be cooked and are therefore only to be used and/or eaten in their raw natural state.

*Although listed in meat and protein grouping, nuts and their butters supply quality essential fats and can be enjoyed in moderation (approximately 1 small handful every other day) within this grouping. Used in this small amount, it will not count against your percentage of daily protein intake.

Spices, Seasonings and Salt

Seasonings, spices and salt can be used to enhance our food and give it additional flavor. However, strong spices like pepper, horseradish, and mustard seed are probably best used sparingly, as these spices may aggrevate a sick individual's weakened condition. When it comes to salt, quality sea salt should be used in contrast to regular table salt, simply because most regular table salt contains aluminum or sugar, both of which are best avoided.

Spices and Seasonings (Use sparingly): All. But use strong spices less frequently.

Sea Salt (About 1 tsp daily): High quality sun-dried sea salts are superior to regular table salt. Check with your physician about what would be a proper level of salt for your particular case.

*Noteably while many people are told to cut down on their salt intake, it is actually needed in small amounts to help the human body function properly. In fact, good quality sea salt is a crucial part of many high fiber vegetarian diets including vegan, macrobiotic, and the McDougall program. Followers of these programs will typically need to add a little more salt while cooking their food due to the drastic reduction of sodium rich foods from their diet. Failure to do so would likely leave these folks feeling weak and unable to properly digest their meals. If this situation is

Christopher K. Sembera (BS, CNC, Be.P)

allowed to continue, serious imbalances could occur which could not only prevent healing but also lead to severe health problems. Nevertheless, even vegetarians and those who reduce sodium rich foods from their diet must learn to consume salt in properly balanced portions, especially those with high or low blood pressure. It is essential that you consult with your physician before deciding how much salt is needed in your diet.

Sweeteners

While these foods can be enjoyed in moderation by those who are in good health, everyone should limit their intake of refined sugars.

Sweeteners (sparingly): stevia, raw unfiltered honey, barley malt, rice syrup, fructose, aspartame, cane syrup, corn syrup, pure maple syrup, blackstrap molasses, and sucrose. Be aware that food processors also sometimes use other words to indicate sugar content in a prepared food. These words include maltose, isomaltose, and dextrose.

*Best choices: stevia, fruit and unsweetened fruit juices are the healthiest choices as sweeteners.

*Next best choices: raw unfiltered honey, blackstrap molasses, rice syrup, and barley malt, fructose syrup or powder, pure maple syrup, cane syrup, sugar, and saccharin.

*Least desirable choices are corn syrup and aspartame. These are best avoided altogether.

Beverages

As with your food, it is recommended that you stay as natural as possible. Raw vegetable juices and pure spring water are your best bets. Bancha, Mu, Kukicha, as well as caffeine-free herbal teas are excellent. Drinks that contain additives, caffeine, sugar, or alcohol are best avoided by the sick, but may be enjoyed in moderation by the healthy.

BEST CHOICES: Beverages (drink whenever thirsty): Spring water (Mountain Valley Water is best), freshly made vegetable juices, low or non-caffeinated herbal teas like bancha (green), mu, kukicha, peppermint and grain teas are best. Likewise, freshly made fruit juices and unsweetened commercial fruit juices both of which are diluted 50% with good quality water are also good.

Your next best bets are mineral water, club soda, decaffeinated coffee and caffeinated herbal teas.

Sports drinks are loaded with sugar and are not a great choice. Still if you have been exposed to extreme heat they are better than risking dehydration and heat stroke. If you have the opportunity to make your own juices, the best electrolyte replacing drink is the carrot, celery, and spinach blend listed in chapter 16.

Beer, wine, and all other alcoholic beverages, as well as caffeinated coffee, soft drinks and their dietary counterparts are best consumed only in moderation.

Condiments and Accompanying Foods

It should be made clear that some minimally-processed foods and condiments can be part of a healthy eating program. However, as mentioned earlier, many products including sauces, gravies, beverages, canned and frozen foods, pickled products, salad dressings, and condiments tend to contain added sugar and preservatives. In addition, many salad dressings and baked goods are made with trans fatty acid-harboring hydrogenated oils. It is of paramount importance that you read labels and determine which products are additive-free or contain minimal amounts of these substances. Although this task will at first be time-consuming, once you learn which products are acceptable, it will rapidly become second nature.

Snack Foods

Snacks are an important part of our diet which help us to maintain our energy levels. However, it is wise to choose snacks that are both nutritious and provide a steady long- lasting supply of energy. Listed below are several foods which will assist us with that goal. This information will help you stick with your healthful eating plan much more effectively.

BEST CHOICES are nuts, seeds and their butters, fresh and dried fruit, and whole wheat breads.

*Whole grain and/or low sugar desserts, gelatins, protein bars and balanced nutrition bars, and plain or mildly salted popcorn, are your next best bets.

<u>*Energy bars are not as good as the protein or balanced bars but are still typically better than candy.</u>

Snacks that are best eaten only on occassion and in moderation include candies, cakes, pies, cookies, marshmellow pies (moon pies), potato chips, corn chips, buttered movie popcorn, cheetos, twinkees, cup cakes and other cream cakes, and most other desserts and junk food goodies.

Serving Sizes

The size of food portions are also important. Proper portion sizes vary from person to person depending upon several factors. In general, those with cardiovascular difficulties are more likely to need a diet which requires 12-15 percent protein. Whereas, individuals who are emaciated and are trying to rebuild their bodies, especially those with gastrointestinal problems, will typically require higher levels of protein. However, this can still vary depending on a number of factors which includes but is not limited to an individual's health status, size, gender and activity level. For help in determining the best approach for your situation, discuss this matter with your physician and nutritional consultant.

Super Foods

Next, I have listed four different groups of foods which are extremely rich in nutrients or that possess a number of beneficial elements which could have a profound impact on health. Each of these can be consumed in food form but have also been converted to supplement form for sake of convenience. I strongly recommend that you become familiar with these special foods and consider using them to help improve the quality of your life. However before doing so, it is suggested that you check with your physician to help determine if these foods can be advantageous to your overall well-being.

Green Foods

The green super foods include wheat grass, yaeyama chlorella, and barley green. All of these are very rich in chlorophyll, vitamins, minerals, amino acids, and have the ability to cleanse our bodies especially the gastrointestinal tract. Two excellent green superfoods are Bio-Green by *Bio-Active* and Chlorella by *Earthrise*. Although each of these foods are excellent possessing many healing benefits, they all have their own unique nutritional composition and provide slightly different advantages. To help determine which green food is best for your case seek the guidance of your doctor and nutritional consultant.

Bee Pollen (OPTIONAL)

Bee pollen is the powder that makes up the male elements of the flower. It is collected and carried by the honey bees back to the hive where it is combined with a small portion of nectar making it easier to store. In the hive, it is used as food for the bees serving as a powerful source of energy. Fortunately for us, bee pollen can also boost our energy levels, as well as provide a tremendous array of nutrients. Its contents include numerous elements such as vitamins A, B-complex, C, D, E, F, K, most amino acids including the eight essential amino acids, most minerals, plant hormones, lecithin, and many enzymes necessary for good health and vitality. It also has natural antibiotic factors helpful for detoxifying the body of many mild forms of bacteria. **The amount used can range from 1 teaspoon to 2 tablespoons; however, it is best to start out slowly and make certain that you are not allergic to it.** According to Dr. Alfred Vogel, author of *The Nature Doctor*, people who have high blood pressure or an overactive thyroid should avoid bee pollen until their problem has been eliminated. Likewise, diabetics, hypoglycemics, pregnant women, those with intestinal diseases, allergy sufferers, and anyone with an existing health problem should also consult with their physician before using bee pollen. For more information on this interesting food see Carlson Wade's two books, *Health from the Hive* and *Bee Pollen and Your Health*.

Bovine Colostrum (OPTIONAL)

Properly gathered bovine colostrum is in my opinion, the greatest natural healing food available. It is a powerful infection fighter, immune system balancer and enhancer, anti-inflammatory, and anti-aging supplement. Because of its broad effectiveness, it is being used to help with a vast number of problems such as persistent infections, intestinal maladies, immune and autoimmune disorders, as well as inflammatory ailments. It also contains growth and healing factors that speed up the healing process of virtually all illnesses.

Colostrum is the pre-milk fluid excreted from the breast of females shortly after birth. Since it is impossible to obtain sufficient amounts from humans, adults can obtain it from organically-raised New Zealand dairy cows. It is essential that high- quality colostrum capsules be used or else you will get little or no benefit. To find the names of companies that produce effective colostrum write the Center for Nutritional Research, 4700 South 900 East, Suite #30-257, Salt Lake City, Utah 84117.

Although colostrum has no known side effects for adults, it is best that you discuss this matter with your physician prior to use. This is especially true for children and pregnant or lactating women. If you desire to learn more about bovine colostrum read the fascinating book, *Colostrum, Life's First Food* by Daniel G. Clark, M.D., and Kaye Wyatt.

In Conclusion

Rather than striving for second best, an **optimum eating plan** provides informative guidelines which empower the individual to preserve peak health in body, mind and spirit. The eating plan should also permit sufficient variety and flexibility, that allows it to be adjusted and meet the needs of carnivores, vegetarians, or semi-vegetarians. As you now know, no single eating plan will be right for everyone. **It is thus absolutely necessary that every eating program be structured to meet the needs of each individual. This is especially true for those who are ill and have special requirements.** Once the correct eating strategy is used, you should literally be able to eat your way to a fit, healthy body. To learn which approach is best for you, it is suggested that you seek the assistance of your physician and nutritional consultant.

Key Points

1. Eat whole grains rather than refined grains.
2. Consume cold pressed "cis" oils rather than hydrogenated "trans fatty" acids.
3. Significantly reduce or eliminate your intake of the health reducers: sugar, food additives, caffeine, alcohol, cigarettes, fluoridated water, improperly used prescription drugs, and illegal drugs.
4. Eat fresh, locally grown, whole foods whenever possible.
5. Eat a wide variety of foods to prevent boredom.
6. Center your diet around whole grains, vegetables, and fruit.
7. Drink one pint of freshly made raw vegetable juice daily or use dark green products like: Greening Power, Bio-Green, or yaeyama chlorella.
8. Eat five or more servings of fiber-rich foods daily.
9. Enjoy your new lifestyle, for it has the potential to assist you in feeling and looking better.

Christopher K. Sembera (BS, CNC, Be.P)

CHAPTER 10

MAXIMIZING DIGESTION

When you eat while working or when you're under stress, you miss out in yet another way: You digest your food less effectively...Dean Ornish, M.D.

Proper digestion is one of the most overlooked factors of health. If one is attempting to get one's body working at its highest level, then it is necessary to first possess a digestive system that is functioning optimally. A healthy digestive system will effectively break down food, absorb nutrients, and cleanse the body. Maximizing the digestive process is a valuable tool for improving health and well-being. However, most of us tend to sidestep this strategy. We instead generally eat very rapidly, hardly chewing the food that we cram into our mouths. When eating in this manner, large chunks of poorly chewed food enter into the gastrointestinal tract. Then, the digestive system is forced to spend lots of energy attempting to breakdown these large food particles. The body is then often unable to nourish properly and cleanse itself in the most proficient way possible. To remedy this situation, I recommend the use of these four strategies:

1. **proper mastication;**
2. **eating foods in an orderly manner;**
3. **consuming more digestive enzymes; and**
4. **abstaining from eating three hours before bedtime.**

The first thing that must be done to help maintain a rock solid digestive system is to thoroughly masticate or chew one's food. Human beings possess three main pairs of salivary glands, the parotid, sublingual, and submandibular. These salivary glands aid in digestion by secreting large amounts of the carbohydrate digesting enzyme amylase (ptyalin). Proper digestion requires that carbohydrates be united with our amylase-rich saliva, which can be best accomplished through proper chewing. As our teeth tear the food down, amylase attacks and begins to digest carbohydrates much more readily. Even the healthiest of people should chew each mouthful of food a minimum of 20 times. Doing so helps to optimize the early stages of the digestive process and enables your gastrointestinal organs to operate more effectively.

Eating in an orderly manner assists the digestive process. Orderly eating means that we should start each meal with our protein-rich or salty foods, and then consume the carbohydrates afterward. According to nutritionist and author, Paavo Airola, in his book, *How To Get Well*, this strategy works because all sodium and protein-rich foods help to stimulate abundant amounts of hydrochloric acid in the stomach, which is needed for proper protein digestion. Eating these foods at the beginning of a meal benefits digestion because hydrochloric acid will be present in generous amounts to breakdown the salty and protein-rich foods. Carbohydrates need less hydrochloric acid for digestion, and so are best eaten toward the end of a meal or at least not prior to the salty and protein foods. Although this technique may seem odd at first, it should pay big dividends to the individual who employs it.

An additional strategy for improving the digestive process is to eat more foods that contain digestive enzymes. Foods such as raw fruit, vegetables and their juices, plus germinated and fermented foods supply the body with additional enzymes to carry out its internal chores. These enzymes reduce the workload that our pancreas would otherwise be required to do. Not only would the pancreas be working harder to convert metabolic enzymes into digestive enzymes, but metabolic enzymes would be robbed from the rest of the body. According to Dr. Edward Howell, author of *Enzyme Nutrition*, the heart, brain, liver, and all organs and tissues end up suffering from an enzyme labor shortage. This can lead to a host of problems, particularly fatigue. For those who need additional enzymes, supplements might be helpful or even necessary. However, before adding an enzyme supplement to your shopping list, check with a nutritional consultant or nutritionally-oriented physician to help determine if you would benefit from one of these products.

Another excellent principle is to abstain from eating three hours before retiring for the night. Failure to comply with this standard can result in two significant problems. First, it can lead to poor digestion, as the meal has not had sufficient time to complete the early digestive process before going to bed. When this occurs, the digestive system will be unable to complete its tasks optimally, likely leading to stagnation and gastrointestinal bloating. By adhering to this rule these types of digestive disturbances can be prevented.

In addition, one's sleeping pattern should also be aided by following this strategy, because the body will not be working overnight trying to digest its last meal. Instead, the body will be free to have a night of undisturbed sleep. It is vital to adhere to this recommendation and avoid late night meals or bingeing.

Conclusion

Properly used, these tools can noticeably improve the functioning of your digestive system and overall health. Compliance with these strategies should also increase energy levels. It is important to utilize these tactics regularly to enhance the digestive system. Then one should have boundless energy to vigorously pursue one's most cherished passions.

Key Factors

1. Eat protein rich and/or salt foods at the beginning of the meal.
2. Eat more foods that contain digestive enzymes.
3. Chew food thoroughly before swallowing.
4. Abstain from eating three hours before retiring.

CHAPTER 11

ENVIRONMENT

The people, places, and things we associate with will have a profound impact on who we shall become...Napoleon Hill

Our environment includes not only our physical surroundings but also everyone we know and everything with which we come into contact. As these diverse elements converge, they contribute to our growth and help determine our future. Therefore, if we desire vibrant health, we should establish an environment that is conducive to encouraging its development. To achieve this, we must properly address the five main components of a healing environment. These elements include associating with supportive people, acquiring a beneficial education, maintaining an orderly home environment, utilizing stress reduction techniques, and reducing our chemical exposures. Consistently applied, these tactics can assist us in creating a wholesome habitat necessary for fostering optimum wellness.

SUPPORTIVE PEOPLE

Supportive people include encouraging spouses, relatives, friends, or just amiable people that you encounter in everyday life. These individuals are beneficial to us because they tend to be optimistic and willing to assist us in the direction of our best interests. They do this for two main reasons. First, they are our true friends and honestly want to see us succeed. Second, these folks understand that if they treat others with kindness and respect, they will receive the same in return. This cycle of good deeds will be to the advantage of everyone involved, as all participants will inevitably be assisted on their own personal journeys.

Furthermore, as supportive people tend to be more optimistic than non-supportive folks they will also be more likely to provide us with lots of healing, positive encouragement. Clearly, this is very helpful, especially when we are having one of our more challenging days. It is strongly suggested that you keep this in mind when selecting the people with whom you will associate.

The penalty for not associating with uplifting people will in all likelihood be prevention from attaining your goals, because the people in our environment will invariably have a great deal of influence over us. Before we can hope to benefit from this strategy, we must first become the type of person that attracts supportive individuals.

EDUCATION

While it is true that one's educational background will usually have a huge impact on his ability to succeed, it is also clear that our level of nutritional knowledge can dramatically influence our overall well-being. Because of this, nutritionally educated individuals are more capable of improving their health, opposed to those who are nutritionally illiterate. It is imperative that you sufficiently arm yourself with the necessary information to achieve a sound physical existence.

Attaining this task can be assisted by keeping abreast of the latest nutritional information. While most of these reports are accurate and properly show the influence nutrition has over health related matters, many others come to conclusions which dispute well-accepted nutritional data.

One such report came out of Finland in the mid-1990s. At the time of its release, it was cited as one of the most thorough and accurate studies on vitamin supplements to date. However, when the results came out, the Finnish study came to some rather odd conclusions. It asserted that antioxidant vitamins A and E provided no protection against lung cancer and even claimed that rates of cancer had increased in those who had taken vitamin A supplements. Interestingly, some critical points about the individuals in the survey were strangely overlooked. For example, the participants of this study were long-time smokers between the ages of 50-69, and had on average smoked at least a pack of cigarettes daily over the past 36 years. Obviously these people were already in the high risk category for cancer due to their unhealthy lifestyles. Some of these people may have had cancer developing in their bodies long before participating in this experiment. Moreover, the dosages of vitamins A and E used was too low to provide any real benefit to the test subjects. These factors made the study virtually useless. In spite of this, the study got a great deal of publicity, although the report told only partial truths and did not contain all pertinent information necessary for a proper assessment. One noteworthy point was that the people who had taken the vitamin E supplements displayed a 36 percent reduction in prostate cancer; curiously, this was hardly mentioned.

The simple reality is that you are responsible for learning the entire truth. Otherwise you can very easily be misled by industries and special interests who are striving to push their agendas. The only way you can be confident about what information to believe is by becoming knowledgeable on all key health-related issues. In this way, you will be prepared to make wise lifestyle choices which are conducive to building a healthy existence.

I suggest that everyone read three books written by experts in the field of nutrition and wellness. *For listings on publications relating to nutrition and wellness, see the rear of this book for my index of suggested readings.* Other good sources of information include the nutritional health magazines like *Natural Health, Delicious, Better Nutrition for Today's Living, Prevention,* and *Let's Live,* all of which can provide a plethora of useful data.

REDUCTION OF UNNECESSARY CHEMICAL EXPOSURE

Modern civilization has uncountable technological advantages and services that are provided to its inhabitants. Yet these advances are not without their drawbacks. One of the more harmful effects is the excessive usage of chemicals in our modern society to which we are exposed.

A vital issue in this area is the usage of chemicals in the production of our food. Environmental physicians have long been concerned with this and continue to stress that we must try to reduce our exposure to these substances. However, altering this approach is not high on the list of farmers and ranchers who utilize chemicals in their production processes. Further, after these foods and their by-products are harvested, more chemicals or preservatives are added for the purpose of increasing their lifespan. Many of these substances can be extremely deleterious, especially for those who are already in a weakened state.

One way to avoid some of these poisons is to buy organically grown foods, which are available at many health food stores as well as some traditional grocery stores. Buying organically grown foods will be more expensive, but they tend to contain fewer pesticides and other chemicals. If you choose not to buy organic foods, wash your fruits and vegetables thoroughly. You should also remove all excess fat from meat and poultry, since this is where most of the steroids and antibiotics used in raising animals will be stored. In this way, you should be able to significantly reduce your exposure to the substances which are frequently present in our food supply.

Another questionable practice that brings discomfort to the chemically sensitive individual is the application of fluoride to water. Although many others may initially seem unaffected by fluoridation, continuous exposure could eventually contribute to the development of a weakened skeletal system. Therefore, it is wise to buy spring or some type of purified water for home usage. According to Dr. Rogers, *Mountain Valley Water* is currently regarded as the finest spring water available.

Chemicals are contained in some toiletries and household cleaners. Toiletries include soap, makeup, deodorant, toothpaste, shampoo, skin and hair-care products. Chemically-free, natural hygiene, cleaning and cosmetic products can be found at most large health food stores and health oriented mail-order companies. These products are generally well-tolerated by even the most sensitive people. If you choose to buy any of these items from a grocery store, it is recommended that you read labels and purchase those which contain the fewest chemical ingredients.

By reducing your intake of chemicals, you will lessen your body's internal work load. In turn, your body will have more energy to spend on the ever important activities like detoxification, healing, and repair. As a result, you may be able to enjoy a healthier and more robust life than you ever dreamed possible.

STRESS REDUCTION

Stress is an inevitable reality of life which will always be present. Nonetheless, how effectively we handle it can make a major difference in whether we attain or fall short of our wellness goal(s). Stress can come in many forms surfacing under certain situations, such as pressure on the job or school, extreme fear, nutritional deficiencies, and illness. Although it would be impractical to eliminate all forms of stress, reduction is something from which everyone would benefit. Along with proper diet and exercise, other pressure- diminishing strategies are meditation, time management, and having an enjoyable career.

MEDITATION/REFLECTION

According to Lawrence LeShan, author of *How To Meditate*, "We meditate to find, to recover, to come back to something of ourselves we once dimly and unknowingly had and have lost without knowing what it was or where or when we lost it." In essence, meditation is a self-evaluation process that enables us to understand more about our inner self and its relation to the world in which we live. Using this self-discovery technique, is also quite helpful in solving internal problems and reducing pressures associated with human life. It does this by enabling us to relax and see through a less emotionally charged perspective, so that we can more effectively address our daily difficulties. Meditation need not take a great deal of time; ten to fifteen minutes of daily contemplation can effectively reduce the strain of modern living. No rigid format need be followed to benefit, only that you silently reflect on some question or circumstance that is producing anxiety, fear, stress, or depression.

To get started, simply ask yourself clear goal specific questions. These questions can include: "Where am I going? What do I want to do with the rest of my life? Will my actions bring me closer to or further away from my objective?" These types of queries can be used to help reflect calmly and examine your current situation, as well as determine which direction your are moving. Invariably, this will allow us to see some of the different options and potential solutions to our circumstances. Then it is up to us to take the required action steps toward the direction of our goals.

It is absolutely necessary that any and all self-analysis exercises be judgment-free. Judging may cause you to engage in self-defeating inner dialogue, which could aid in lowering your self-concept. If this occurs you will not gain from reflection but instead be negatively affected by it.

A model program that teaches people how meditation can be helpful for managing stress is taught by Dr. Jon Kabat-Zinn's Stress Reduction and Relaxation Program at the University of Massachusetts Medical Center. Dr. Kabat-Zinn claims that one of the biggest benefits of his program is that people are taught to understand that their worrisome thoughts are just worrisome thoughts, not reality. In so doing, people are then better able to deal with anxiety and all the physiological effects which it brings. For additional information on this program, read Dr. Kabat-Zinn's book, *Full Catastrophe Living*.

We now understand that meditation/reflection can be used to help relieve our daily stresses, as well as improve one's internal mental outlook. Properly used it enables the user to clearly and harmlessly view his or her circumstances and determine what can be done to improve matters. To gain benefit, the individual must consistently utilize this technique to restructure efforts in the direction of one's aspirations. Thus, one will not only increase one's mental awareness but also reduce emotional and physiological tension, enabling one to experience life in a more relaxed, peaceful state.

TIME MANAGEMENT

One of the greatest success tools in any endeavor is proper time management. The reason for this is that without good time management skills, you will probably never have the time to perform all the vital actions which are required for success. It is essential that you learn to properly prioritize and structure your life around activities which assist the attainment of your most prized goals.

Two of the finest time management programs are *How To Get Control Of Your Time And Your Life* by Alan Lakein, and *How To*

Master Your Time by Brian Tracy. The one key factor that these two men and all other organizational experts emphasize is prioritizing. As was discussed in chapter 5, prioritizing simply means organizing your life in conjunction with your values. After doing so, you then must focus the vast majority of your time on the activities that will bring the greatest long-term payoffs. At that point, if you have time remaining, you can use it on the less important tasks. In other words, since there is never enough time to do everything, you must instead make certain that you complete the essentials first. Then, if you do not have time for the less important things, you have missed relatively little.

ENJOYABLE CAREER

Although this seems to be a very obvious factor in one's personal environment, many people never invest sufficient time to decide which career path they will choose. This lack of preparation likely contributes to much of the vocational dissatisfaction and negative mental attitudes that surround work in today's society. Interestingly, motivational experts claim that only three percent of all Americans have completed clearly written goals. Yet this small percentage earns on average 10 times more than the other 97 percent. The reason for the goal-setter's success is obvious. These people have taken the necessary time to determine their path and prioritize their lives. These folks usually end up working in a field that they enjoy and approach their career with an attitude of positive expectancy rather than as a dreaded reality.

Several books and programs exist to assist you in choosing your career path. Paul and Barbara Tieger's book, *Do What You Are,* is one such example. Other good sources for this information include the Nightingale-Conant Corporation, libraries, and your local bookstore.

To help with the career selection process, you should ask yourself questions like: How can I best provide service to others? What would I like to do with my life? If I had unlimited time, talent, and money what would I do with my life? If I won the lottery, would I continue working in my current field of employment?

Questions such as these tend to bring out into the open your true vocational aspirations. After you have determined your career path, goal-setting exercises can aid you in developing a plan of action to pursue your heart's desire. As a result of this process, your chances of working in a field that you love become dramatically more likely.

A HAPPY HOME

Another key element of a healthy environment is a pleasant home. A well-organized clean house is not only a nice place to live in, but it is also conducive to creating a more peaceful, healthy existence. Two key components exist in creating and maintaining a healing home: keeping it clean and neat, as well as using an air-purifier.

It is always best to live in a clean, orderly home. This will allow you the luxury of living in a setting which limits clutter and household allergens like dust and pollen. Taking, this step will make your time at home more relaxing and less stressful.

Many allergy sufferers believe that the use of a HEPA filter and/or air-purifier is invaluable for cleaning the air of incoming pollutants. A HEPA filter can easily be added to your air-conditioning system and for relatively little cost. However, these filters are only effective when the air-conditioning system is in use. In contrast, air-purifiers are more costly but run continuously and are more aggressive at preventing the accumulation of indoor allergens. Most advocates of purifiers recommend that they be utilized in the bedroom, thus you will be breathing clean purified air for approximately 1/3 of your day. This should help you to wake up feeling well-rested and refreshed. If you wish to purchase one or both of these cleaning systems, see your local retail stores and/or health store outlets.

Conclusion

Certainly, the environment in which we live affects whether or not we will experience a healthy, happy life. In order to enhance our environment, it is essential that we utilize the five factors which were discussed in this chapter. We can then create the type of surroundings which are necessary for achieving optimum levels of wellness.

Key Factors

1. Bring supportive, loving people into your life.
2. Educate yourself on all health-related matters.
3. Avoid toxic people, places, and things whenever possible.
4. Learn how to reduce and manage stress.
5. Make your home a healthy, loving, positive environment.

Christopher K. Sembera (BS, CNC, Be.P)

CHAPTER 12

EXERCISE

"The sovereign invigorator of the body is exercise." Thomas Jefferson

Without question this is one of America's most commonly recommended health strategies as evidence in the large number of health and fitness training facilities. Nonetheless, in spite of its widespread availiability, a recent report indicates that only 25 percent of all Americans are exercising on a regular basis. While some people may be physically unable to exercise, many more are just simply choosing not to engage in physical activity. If you wish to improve in this area, you must begin by changing your way of thinking about exercise. This is accomplished by selecting training routines that you enjoy, and by easing slowly into these regimens at your own pace. If these measures are followed, you will be much more likely to live a physically active lifestyle.

Before getting started many of us are forced to face our internal fears and admit to ourselves just how out of shape we really are. Facing this reality can be difficult, but acknowledging this point is frequently the first obstacle that must be overcome. After these fears are confronted, you can then be freed from your inner defenses to pursue your optimum fitness level.

The other crucial aspect of exercise is consistency. Consistency, which is the key to long lasting fitness, is absolutely necessary if you are to achieve and maintain long-term health. Your body needs steady physical activity. When you engage in regular exercise your body's requirements for activity are fulfilled. As a result, your body functions better and becomes healthier.

Along with enhancing one's quality of life, exercise has been used to help with a vast array of disorders like depression, high cholesterol, fatigue, toxemia, heart disease, and obesity, to name a few. Exercise is effective, because it stimulates all bodily organs to function at a higher level. According to author and fitness educator, Covert Bailey, "exercise makes demands on every organ in the body." Mr. Bailey cites several examples, stating that exercise causes the liver to produce glycogen more efficiently, the pancreas regulates insulin and glucose more effectively, and the level of LDL (harmful) cholesterol in the blood drops, while the HDL (beneficial) cholesterol ascends. Exercise is thus a necessary part of building health.

For those of you who are in the non-exercising group and wish to change, you might want to start by walking briskly 30 minutes, four to six days per week. Of all exercises that are currently discussed, this is likely the most widely recommended activity by experts in the health and wellness industry. Fitness authority, Kathy Smith, calls walking the no-excuse workout and cites it as an ideal exercise for people of all ages. She also claims that when consistency and speed are combined with walking, a plethora of payoffs occur, such as cardiovascular benefits, disease prevention, longevity, improved life quality, psychological benefits, increased energy, muscle toning, and weight control. The reasons for walkings' popularity are obvious. It is simple, inexpensive and much safer than many other forms of exercise. Walking is an exercise that most people find relatively easy to stick with, for the simple reason that they enjoy doing it.

The benefits of walking were noted several years ago by Dr. David Brandt, who found that even moderate amounts of walking could have a dramatic impact on health. Dr. Brandt confirmed this when he took men who had elevated blood fat levels and asked them to walk two miles in 30 minutes four times per week. The men who participated in this program made no dietary changes. Still, three weeks into the program, the men saw their average blood fat levels fall almost 60 percent, bringing them within the normal range. To make certain that walking caused this reduction, the program was discontinued for five weeks. The result was that the participants' blood fat levels went back up to their original high levels. This example clearly demonstrates that even moderate exercising can be tremendously advantageous.

Although I have emphasized walking, there are other exercise activities which can help you to experience many of the same benefits associated with brisk walking. These can include bike riding, jogging, and the use of certain fitness equipment like a step machine. While proper usage of the various aerobic training equipment does provide a good number of the same payoffs as does outdoor activity, I still find it more desirable to get out into the fresh air.

Other good exercise activities include tennis, racquetball, swimming, and hiking. Much of the conventional wisdom now recommends that you do a wide variety of these activities so that you can: work to train your entire body and prevent boredom. In this way, you may be able to keep your workouts both fun and effective.

It is also very important that you keep a proper balance of strength, flexibility and endurance activities in your exercise regimen. These three elements allow the entire body to get a complete workout. Strength training which increases muscular development includes weight lifting, nautilus machines, and isometric exercises. Flexibility work focuses on bending and stretching to loosen up those muscles and joints. While endurance routines include walking, jogging, tennis, hiking, swimming, biking, and step aerobics. By incorporating a wide range of these activities into your training regimen, you can build a strong well-functioning body for all of lifes' challenges.

An endless supply of valuable exercise information abounds in the various book and video stores. Two of my favorite books on this topic are Covert Bailey's, *Smart Exercise,* and Kathy Smith's, *Walk Fit.* While Mr. Bailey's book is very informative on the physiological benefits of exercise, Ms. Smith's, *Walk Fit,* is an excellent source for learning how to exercise safely and effectively.

Ultimately, the key to exercise is that you do it regularly, because only when exercise is consistent will you receive long-term benefits. Probably the best place to start is with a 30 minute brisk walk, which when done four to six times per week will supply many of the benefits of vigorous exercise. If you decide to add other exercise regimens to your daily walk, then all the better. It is best you choose something that you enjoy, and remember to adjust your routine periodically to prevent boredom. Before starting with any exercise program check with your physician to determine what regimen will be the most appropriate for you and your bodys' needs.

Key Factors

1. Consistently walk 30 minutes per day at a brisk pace.
2. Maintain a proper balance of endurance, flexibility, and strength activities in your exercise regimen.
3. Choose exercises that you enjoy; otherwise, you may become bored and discontinue this magnificent health strategy.

Christopher K. Sembera (BS, CNC, Be.P)

CHAPTER 13

HEREDITY

We all have the ability to choose the type of environment that will impact our basic genetics...Jeffrey Bland., Ph.D.

According to *Webster's Universal Dictionary and Thesaurus*, heredity is the transmission of genetic material that determines physical and mental characteristics from one generation to another. Clearly our genetic matter is of great significiance and has a role in deciding our health status. It is my contention that our upcoming years will be determined by how effectively we nourish the needs of our body, mind, and spirit. Meaning that although we may possess genetic tendencies to certain health problems, we are usually not predestined to develop these ailments. It is instead our lifestyle that provides the decisive factor as to whether we will succumb to disease or live a hearty existence. It is therefore imperative that we work to satisfy our body's requirements.

Before this can be achieved, one must first recognize and accept these four basic principles. First is understanding that while genetics play a role in our future, lifestyle improvements may negate many health problems from ever occurring. Second, we must be aware that scientists tend to provide documentation which support the desired conclusions of society. Third, is our awareness that the greatest limits which we possess are those we place on ourselves; and finally that each individual will always retain his or her genetic tendencies. These principles encourage an understanding that is required to initiate and complete the healing process.

Although dietary and lifestyle improvements prevent many health problems before they happen, prevention continues to be underutilized. Many health experts agree that leading a healthy lifestyle could safeguard against most cases of disease and illness. While I am of the opinion that this figure is very conservative, it still serves to signal us that we should be taking better care of bodies. In fact, when diet and exercise regimens are employed consistently people usually feel better, are more energetic, and in some cases even rebuild their health. The simple reality is that the majority of people who suffer with chronic illnesses live predominately on refined foods and lead inactive, unwholesome lives. Chronic and degenerative diseases are far less common in areas where people subsist on unrefined foods. Interestingly, when these people are brought to America and put on our highly refined diet, they tend to develop health disorders at about the same rates that we do.

It is my firm opinion that this occurs because one's way of life is the main ingredient that contributes to our state of health. According to biologist and author, Ruth Hubbard, "Inherited factors can have an impact on our health, but their effects are embedded in a network of biological and ecological relationships." Because of these various health factors, it is essential that we not overemphasize the connection between genetics and disease. Instead, we should focus more on the environmental aspects, especially those that we can actually improve upon. In this way, we can help prevent illnesses and achieve a high level of physical well-being.

Scientific studies tend to provide results which support the beliefs and values of society. One of the most powerful examples of scientific manipulation occurred in the 1800s, when some scientists came to the conclusion that schooling damaged girls' reproductive organs. They further concluded that this could prevent them from bearing children. As a result of this nonsense, young girls were deprived from getting the same educational opportunities as boys. Obviously, this was a foolish theory that actually hurt our country, as it prevented some women from fully developing into the people that they would have become. However, this silly view prevailed because it was consistent with the ideology of the public at that time. This outrageous example distinctively shows just how far some scientists have gone in the past to defend societal beliefs.

It is my concern, that we may have a similar problem today with some geneticists over-emphasizing the connection between genes and disease. Many health advocates share my view and believe that the genetic-disease link is being exaggerated. John McDougall, M.D., in his book, *The McDougall Program*, says that according to his experience, genetically caused illnesses are exceedingly rare. Similarly, Robert Kradjian, M.D., author of *Save Yourself from Breast Cancer*, has concluded that breast cancer is primarily an environmental disease and not a genetic disease as taught in medical school. In sharp contrast to some health care professionals, these doctors cite diet and other lifestyle (environmental) factors as being the key elements which typically determine our health status. While there are exceptions to this point, my argument is that we are not effectively focusing on the role of diet and healthy living. When this occurs, we can easily be diverted from a real opportunity to improve our health. We must instead realize that in most cases we have a real chance to shape and mold our own destiny. This is certainly a much more optimistic approach than the hopeless and negative outlook which suggests that we cannot improve upon our health situation.

Although genetic limitations exist, the greatest boundaries that humans possess are those we place on ourselves. These mental obstacles result from our past experiences, which laid the groundwork for our belief system. Meaning that if we have been victorious in the past, we grow to anticipate success in the future. The opposite is also accurate; if we have been unsuccessful, then we tend to expect failure. Because of this pattern of defeat, underachievers wind up creating mental limitations that obstruct them from attaining their objectives. The tragedy here is that many of the so-called barriers to success often exist only in their imagination.

Before these people can be helped, they must first understand that their lack of confidence is not the result of a genetic deficiency. Their problem is based on their earlier experiences, which cause them to fear that they will again fail. This fear is a natural emotion that we all experience at one time or another. It frequently appears when we are afraid of trying a new approach or something that we were previously unable to achieve. **One key to getting over this fear is to admit to yourself that you are afraid.** You should then be able to evaluate your concern with greater clarity, so that you can begin to look for solutions to your situation. The difficulty is that most people do not want to admit their fears and even try to cover them up with phony excuses. Examples of this would include: "That's just the way

I am;" or "I was born this way." These statements are used by the person to protect his weakened self-image. Protective or defense mechanisms like these are very self-limiting and thus prevent one from effectively addressing their problems.

To advance from this point, you must instead develop and utilize a success-oriented mentality. In this way, you will have a realistic opportunity to break the cycle of repeated failure. Achieving this assignment necessitates that you introduce some activities which will allow you to experience success. Simply because, nothing succeeds like success. Once done, you will be able to reverse self-defeating patterns of thinking and replace them with newfound optimism for the future.

The key aspect of this principle and our self-advancement is believing that while we retain inherited tendencies, we still have the power to alter our future. Rather than blaming our situation on a genetic weakness, we should trust that our goals can be achieved. In this way, we can effectively rid ourselves of the false belief that we have no control over our health and well-being. Dr. Wayne Dyer said it best in his book *The Sky's The Limit*, ***"A high level of mental and physical health is available for anyone who is willing to go after it, and no one has any better chance of becoming more self-actualized or more fully functioning than anyone else."*** So what are you waiting for? Strive for and achieve your optimum level of health and well-being.

The final element of this strategy is accepting that the genetic tendencies we inherit will remain until death. It never ceases to amaze me how many people cannot seem to understand this basic rule. This is perfectly illustrated by people who are well on the way to recovery from a major illnesses, yet are unable to adhere to their healing plan after improvement is noted. Although these folks initially make significant lifestyle enhancements, they are apparently unwilling to stay the course and instead choose to place themselves in situations which leave them vulnerable to their inherited weaknesses. In so doing, they are failing to understand that their genetic tendencies will always be present and that their new healthy lifestyle is a necessary part of health preservation.

Key to improving your situation is comprehending that our lifestyle intermixes with our heredity and sets the stage for either disease or vitality. Therefore, it is essential that we make the necessary adjustments in our lifestyle to restore and/or sustain our optimum level of wellness. To achieve wellness, it is necessary for many to adhere to strict healing phases of their health enhancing plan. Healing phases, which are for the sick, usually take from 6 months to three years or more depending upon the type and severity of the illness. Only after health has been restored can these folks enjoy some of their old favorites on **occasion** and in **moderation**. Nevertheless, always remember that a complete return to your old habits can lead to a recurrence of your illness. This is why we can never forget that our inherited traits will forever remain a part of our existence.

While some hereditary factors exist which can lead to illness and interfere with healing, these in my view are the exception to the rule and should not be bestowed with any great emphasis. It is instead much more beneficial to use this strategy to focus on improving the environmental factors of health. In this way, we can realize that although our genetic pattern plays an indispensable role in our physical growth and development, it usually does not prevent us from maintaining our health. In reality, it is our way of living which has the greatest impact on our physical and mental well-being. It is thus my recommendation that you not allow any hereditary limitations keep you from achieving your highest level of health. Instead learn what your body and mind need to perform best and live your life accordingly.

Key Factors

1. Dietary and lifestyle changes could thwart many health problems before they occur.
2. Scientific studies often provide results which support beliefs of society.
3. The greatest limits which we possess are those that we place on ourselves.
4. Understand that you will retain your genetic tendencies all of your life.

CHAPTER 14

TAKING ACTION

It doesn't matter how young or how old you are if you want your life to thrive you must have the courage to step into tomorrow...Robert H. Schuller

Throughout this book, I have discussed a number of strategies, all of which are helpful to healing and health maintenance. However, if you do not combine these tactics with positive action steps, then the program is of little or no value. Meaning that along with having knowledge of these strategies you must also utilize them. Because, contrary to popular belief, knowledge is only power when it is combined with action. This can be seen throughout our society, where the vibrantly healthy people are those individuals that actually live healthful lifestyles, opposed to those who are talking about doing so. If you want to achieve wholeness, then you too must live your life engaging in positive actions which will encourage your physical, mental, and spiritual well-being.

Positive actions are seen when we make lifestyle choices which are in contrast to our previous destructive activities. Although facing the unknown and following through with new, healthier approaches can be challenging, it is a necessary part of the growth process. As we go through this process, we will face obstacles that must be overcome if we are to resolve or improve our situation. This objective can only be achieved, by consistently taking positive actions steps to defeat these obstructions. Therefore, it is imperative that you persistently utilize health building strategies throughout this time and never lose sight of your wellness goals.

This process of growth allows individuals to experience and attain high levels of **hope, faith, and courage**. These qualities are crucial to taking action, because they build confidence and emotionally prepare you to handle the barriers to success. Once achieved, individuals will have an enhanced ability to influence the circumstances in their lives, enabling them to more effectively deal with and even solve their own problems.

HOPE

Hope is what singer Gloria Estefan was referring to in her 1992 hit, *Always Tomorrow*. The lyrics in the song go, "There's always tomorrow to start over again, things will never stay the same, only one sure thing is change, that's why there's always tomorrow." Her primary message in the song is to never give up hope because virtually all things change or can be changed.

Hope is also the one quality that you must never lose; otherwise, there is nothing that you or anyone else can do to help you. In many cases, when all hope is removed many will believe they have no reason to continue living. Not hoping for better living and brighter futures may also cause you to stop searching for new ideas and opportunities. The common result is the creation of an despondent individual who stagnates and becomes pessimistic about one's life as well as the world in which one lives. This has unfortunately become all too typical in our culture.

To stimulate hope, I recommend using the strategy which W. Clement Stone called inverse paranoia. It is the quality of being convinced that a positive conspiracy is present and working to help you accomplish your goals. Use of this tool enables you to develop an optimistic frame of mind and bring into your life those people who will assist you. Properly applied, this concept can help you to look forward to each day with eager anticipation.

However, this mind-set can only be realized if you maintain hope that some benefit can be gained from your actions. In my own case, this was crucial to advancing my health. Because of hope, I never stopped searching for the answers to my health problems. In which case, I was eventually able to find approaches and tools which were beneficial. Then, I adhered to my personal wellness plan and was able to initiate the healing process. This was accomplished because I maintained hope even after years of illness and uncertainty about how to resolve my situation. Living with a hopeful attitude definitely brought many new opportunities and possibilities within my grasp. Thus, if you wish to increase your chances of wholeness, it is necessary that you too remain hopeful of better times.

FAITH

To me faith is simply the act of believing that everything will work out for the best. Achievers in our society are well aware of this quality, as they possess it at great levels. This nourishes their belief that they can accomplish any objective they pursue. In contrast, unsuccessful people are typically lacking in faith. Believing that you will eventually be successful is thus one of the most vital ingredients of a prosperous plan, with which we can conquer nearly every challenge we meet. Or as the *Bible* says, "All things are possible to him who believith."

Self-achievement expert and author Napoleon Hill, claims that many people spend much of their time fearing all the things which they do not want such as illness, poverty, failure, and disease. The result is that many of these folks actually create these very problems in their lives. He claimed that this occurs because our prevailing thoughts tend to manifest themselves in our physical selves. Mr. Hill recommends that you avoid these negative thoughts, and instead spend the majority of your time positively envisioning the things that you want in your life. In so doing, you will be building faith in your ability to reach your goal.

Developing faith requires that you find a reason (definite purpose) for following a healing program and then acquire a burning desire for its achievement. To do this, it is necessary to create a list of health goals that you want to accomplish. (This is the purpose of the upcoming goal setting exercises.) You are then instructed to devise a specific action plan of how you will try to achieve your goals. In so doing, you formulate a defined plan of how you will proceed in trying to improve your overall health. This process fosters a powerful confidence or faith that your listed goals can be achieved. Properly used, this principle will supply you with desire, encouragement, and the necessary faith to make the required positive changes in your life.

Another benefit of the development of faith is that it gives you the ability to let God handle all the problems in this world over which you have no control. After all God is the Master Controller of the Universe, and if the Creator cannot help you then no one can.

COURAGE

The third and final step required for action taking is the development of courage. This is the key ingredient that you must have or obtain to make positive changes in your life. Because after determining your goals, you must then possess the fortitude to follow through with your planned actions. This is very evident in successful people who, when facing tough situations, can assert ample amounts of willpower to address their circumstances. These individuals succeed because they consistently and sufficiently engage in positive actions until their plans succeed. To effectively pursue our goals, we too must demonstrate this type of tenacity. Those who develop strong levels of courage will inevitably become action takers, which will dramatically enhace their chances of succeeding.

To assist with your development, it is suggested that you employ the assistance of two or three people, living or deceased who display the qualities of hope, faith, and courage. All you have to do is imagine what your heroes would say and do if they were in your situation. This tactic will allow you to access the inspirational qualities of these individuals whenever you find yourself lacking in willpower. The result of this activity is that both your emotional psyche and confidence level will receive a boost.

Name two or three people whom you admire that consistently display the qualities of hope, faith, and courage. Plus, list the advice that they would they give you for building these qualities?

1. _____
   _____
   _____
   _____

2. _____

_____
_____
_____
_____

3. _____
_____
_____
_____
_____

When you find yourself in a tough situation, simply follow the advice of your role models.

GOAL SETTING

Now that you have seen the three-step process for becoming an action taker, it is time to begin this process by setting goals. This is the first step in enhancing health because it provides an aiming point for what quality of life you want to experience. It also aids in creating reasons for following a wellness regimen, as everyone has different motivations for wanting to be on a health building program. Maybe you suffer with a recurring ailment, are overweight, lack energy, wish to prevent premature aging, or just want to maximize your overall health. The following exercises are designed to help you develop a wellness plan which should assist you throughout your attempts to attain your goals.

These exercises are in actuality altered versions of the works of personal achievement educators like Zig Ziglar, Anthony Robbins, Brian Tracy, Earl Nightingale, and Napoleon Hill. I came across the works of these men, while trying to find an orderly way to construct my own healing plan. To increase my odds of success, I incorporated these reworked strategies into my healing program. The result was that it enabled me to focus clearly on my goals and see what was needed to reach them. If you are truly serious about healing, I highly recommend that you also use these strategies.

It cannot be understated that your desire to change is absolutely crucial to healing. Therefore, if optimum wellness is your goal, it is your job to take the necessary time to discover within yourself as many reasons as possible for making these enhancements. The good news is that each reason will supply you with more personal motivation for making the essential lifestyle improvements. Whatever reason(s) you have for doing this program are fine, just make sure that your reason(s) motivate you more than all the obstacles that will inevitably be present between you and your goals.

COMMON HEALTH & HAPPINESS GOALS

Below are some of the more common wellness goals (reasons) that people pursue as motivational tools for making lifestyle improvements. Select one or more of these or list your own reason(s).

- Develop clear skin
- Increase energy levels (stamina)
- Prevent premature aging
- Prevent or reduce colds and infections
- Eliminate minor aches and pains
- Longevity
- Improve Health
- Regain and maintain my ideal weight
- Lose weight around midsection
- Lose weight around thighs and buttocks
- Lower cholesterol levels
- Lower blood pressure
- Other _____
  _____
  _____
  _____
  _____
  _____

Come up with as many goals as possible. Remember, that the more reasons that you have for making lifestyle improvements, then the stronger will be your desire to succeed. In addition, make your reasons more vivid by giving specifics on what you will do when your goal is achieved.

Example: (Goal) To increase energy.

(Specifics) So that I can be able to enjoy my free time with family and friends, without experiencing fatigue. This will be extremely enjoyable during weekends when I have more free time for activities like traveling, shopping, dating, and goofing off.

Your Goals and Specifics:_____
_____
_____
_____
_____
_____
_____
_____
_____
_____
_____

OPTIMUM FUNCTIONING

List three times in your life when you were at peak levels of health and fitness. Describe how you felt and how much more effective you were in everything you did.
Be as descriptive as possible, then reflect on how wonderful it would be to feel and live that way again.

Memory # 1: _____
_____
_____
_____
_____
_____
_____

Memory # 2: _____
_____

Christopher K. Sembera (BS, CNC, Be.P)

_____
_____
_____
_____
_____

Memory # 3: _____
_____
_____
_____
_____
_____
_____

PLANNING STEPS

Complete the next fourteen exercises which are designed to guide you through your personal healing experience. The mere act of completing these exercises will start a chain of events which make it far more likely that you will achieve your health goals.

1. List the healthcare professionals that will be assiting you with your healing journey.

   _____
   _____
   _____
   _____

2. Write the dates that you plan to see these people.

   _____
   _____
   _____
   _____

3. Cite the eating plan that you are going to use as a dietary guideline.

   _____

4. Write the date that you will begin this eating plan.
   _____

5. Select and read 3-5 books written by experts in the health and wellness field.
   This will help provide information that you need for reaching your objective(s). List these books below and the dates which you will complete reading these publications.
   _____
   _____
   _____
   _____

6. List the supportive people in your life.
   _____
   _____
   _____
   _____
   _____

* Strategy: Ask loved ones for their support and assistance. Make this experience a time to grow closer to the special people in your life.

7. List days and times that you will spend with your supportive friends and associates. *You may estimate days and times if necessary.*
   _____
   _____
   _____
   _____
   _____
   _____

8. List the people that will likely try to discourage you from your wellness goals.

These individuals can be family, friends, co-workers, or school mates who are not overly enthusiastic or supportive of your new healthy lifestyle.

_____
_____
_____
_____
_____

* Strategy: Spend more time with the helpful supportive people than the non- supportive people.

9. List what you will say to deflect those who will try to distract you from your healthy lifestyle.
   Example, if someone asks you to go out and eat junk food, tell them your health regimen does not allow it but that you will meet them later at the movies, ball game, shopping, etc.

_____
_____
_____
_____
_____
_____

10. List the obstacles that might present themselves between you and your wellness goals. *Examples: non-supportive people, unhealthy environment, bad lifestyle choices, unsatisfying career, poor time management, previous lack of success causes you to doubt your abilities, etc.*

_____
_____
_____
_____
_____
_____

11. **Cite ideas to counteract these distractions.** *Examples: Terminate excess emotional baggage, consolidate some activities, eliminate unnecessary work, end unloving relationships, associate with people who want you to succeed, etc.*

_____
_____
_____
_____
_____
_____
_____

12. **What will you do when self-pity strikes?** *Examples could be to turn on more will power, laugh at yourself, call a supportive friend, focus on and review your goals, think of what your role model would do, etc.*

_____
_____
_____
_____
_____
_____
_____

13. **List any support systems or groups to which you belong and participate.** *Examples include any and all healing support groups.*

_____
_____
_____

14. **List the positive things you will do for yourself once you achieve your objective.** *Example, vacation, shopping, and reflect on all the things for which you are grateful.*

_____
_____
_____
_____
_____
_____

Christopher K. Sembera (BS, CNC, Be.P)

Congratulations on having just completed your game plan for building wellness. These exercises are intended to provide the necessary tools and motivation that you need to counter all the distractions that you will likely encounter. Although goal setting does not guarantee the achievement of your health aspirations, it does dramatically increase your chances of success. Before moving on, make certain to thoroughly complete and review these exercises so that you can increase your opportunities for health enhancement.

Key Factors

1. Action is the key to success.
2. Hope is the beginning of success, because it enables you to keep seeking the answers to your problem(s).
3. Faith, is believing that everything will resolve itself in the end.
4. Courage (applied faith) allows one to pursue his goal in spite of the inevitable obstructions which will always be present.
5. Goal setting is important because it provides an aiming point and the necessary motivation to change.

Now that you have been acquainted with the ten factors of health and happiness, it is up to you to use them. Although these methods promise no guarantee, they have proven to be effective time and time again, and they can work for you as well. Of course to benefit from these strategies, it is necessary that they be employed on a consistent basis. Just remember it's not all or nothing, the more you do the more you will benefit. Ultimately, you have to be the judge about how much of this philosophy you wish to incorporate into your life. Because when all is said and done, you are the one that needs to be comfortable with your choices and overall quality of life.

CHAPTER 15
HELPFUL HINTS

The process of change does not happen easily. It needs to be planned...Paul W. Swets

This chapter is dedicated to supplying you with numerous healthful tips and answers the questions which I am most frequently asked. I have found it necessary to compile this list of tips and data as many of my clients were simply being overwhelmed with all of this health related information. As a result, they were left confused and uncertain as to how they should proceed in terms of implementing this new knowledge into their lives. Fortunately since supplying these details they have had a much easier time in gaining the wisdom necessary for making the transition to a healthier lifestyle. To help you review this data, it has been segmented into five main parts including, (1) health, food, and dietary tips, (2) way of life suggestions, (3) the five flavors, (4) organizational tips, and (5) a question and answer section.

Health, Food, and Dietary Tips

* While some people can thrive on a properly balanced vegetarian diet, many others cannot and feel their best eating some animal protein three or four times per week. Then again some of us may need animal protein every day and at every meal. Listen to your body!

* Beware that strict vegetarians may run the risk of Vitamin B-12 deficiency. Since this can cause serious health problems, it would be wise to eat some B-12 rich, animal protein at least once a week. If the person is unwilling to do this then a B complex supplement containing B-12 is usually strongly recommended. B-12 rich natural supplements like Bio-Green and Greening Power are other viable options.

Christopher K. Sembera (BS, CNC, Be.P)

   * Never begin any healing or health enhancing program without the approval and assistance of a physician and nutritional consultant.

   * If utilizing a health building plan, you should follow it as designed or else new and potentially dangerous imbalances can result.

   * If unable to comply with new lifestyle guidelines, tell your physician and consultant so that adjustments can be made to design a plan which you will follow.

- If a medically trained physician temporarily suggests or approves a high protein, low-carbohydrate diet, it will be necessary to eat significant amounts of vegetables which are low in starch. Some of these vegetables include broccoli, cauliflower, string beans, asparagus, summer squash, greens, turnips, and cabbage. In addition, if carrot, spinach, celery and other vegetable and fruit juices are tolerated, it is recommended that they be consumed daily. Some supplementation is also likely to be necessary; discuss this with your physician and nutritional consultant. For a more detailed listing of acceptable foods, as well as additional information on this type of approach, see Elaine Gottschall's, *Breaking the Vicious Cycle*.

   * If cramping, one may be low in potassium, magnesium, and/or calcium and would likely benefit from fresh vegetable juices. The most beneficial juices would come from carrot, celery, spinach, and parsley. Dark green supplement foods like barley and wheat grass, would also be helpful.

   * After working with raw meat and meat products make certain that you thoroughly wash hands and all surfaces which have had direct or indirect physical contact with these foods.

   * Never use wooden cutting boards when slicing meat and meat products as these boards can absorb moisture and food residue and thus provide a suitable breeding ground for unhealthy bacteria. Plastic cutting boards are a far better choice, as they can be effectively

cleaned after each use so that we can dramatically reduce the risks of mold or fungus buildup.

* White flour, white rice and other refined grains are nutritionally weak foods; choose whole grains and flour products made from whole grains whenever possible.

* Only buy whole wheat breads which list whole wheat or some other whole grain flour as the first ingredient.

* When eating whole grains and whole grain products, chew them at least 20 times to properly breakdown these foods and thus gain the full nutritional benefits.

* The overwhelming majority of all health ailments can be helped by reducing consumption of refined foods and replacing them with unrefined, whole foods.

* Eat enough to maintain your ideal weight, but make sure your food portions are balanced and chew well.

* For those with health disorders looking for a dietary guideline to follow the blood type diet book D'Amato, Eat Right for your type, is an excellent place to start.

* Try to reduce the number of times that you eat out at restaurants, two to three meals per week is a good goal for many. Reduce the number of times eating out even further if possible.

* To heal the body you must first improve the quality of the blood, which is primarily achieved through optimum eating.

* Some people find it desirable to eat two to three meals per day while others feel their best eating four to six smaller meals per day. Choose the approach that is best for you.

* If one is overweight then it is probably best to eat only when hungry.

* Eat organically grown foods when feasible. This is more important for those with weakened immune systems.

* If limiting dairy products, you should eat or juice at least two cups of dark leafy greens each day. It is also essential that you eat plenty of other calcium rich foods like sesame seeds, dark leafy greens, whole grains, vegetables, beans, and fish with bones. In addition, it would be wise to see a nutritional consultant about the possibility of supplementation.

* Vegetarians and semi-vegetarians should make certain to eat whole grain cereals and their products rather than the refined grain products. Otherwise, they could be laying the foundation for nutritional deficiencies.

* Avoid margarine and vegetable shortening whenever possible, instead use cold pressed olive oil or on occasion, small amounts of unsalted butter.

* Most commercial salad dressings, snack and dessert foods use partially hydrogenated oils, which contain trans fatty acids. It is best to avoid or limit these products. You should be able to find many alternative products at health food stores which use cold or expeller pressed oils.

* Be aware that most low or non-fat commercial salad dressings also contain high levels of refined sugar. This is just another reason to make your own dressing or buy a healthier version.

* Use high quality sea salt, not table salt. Table salt contains aluminum, which has been indicated as a possible contributor to Alzheimer's disease. Kosher salt may also be an acceptable alternative.

* If you have dramatically reduced your consumption of sodium rich, refined foods and are now eating more whole, unrefined vegetable foods, make certain that you add back enough sea salt.

Otherwise, you will likely feel weak and be unable to function properly. Check with your physician and nutritional consultant to determine an appropriate level.

* When consuming extremely expansive foods like sugar, caffeine, alcohol, tobacco, or prescription drugs, it is important that they be balanced with a sufficient amount of contractive foods. Contractive foods include meat, eggs, seafood, and sea salt. Otherwise, you could knock your body out of equilibrium leading to health disturbances.

* Whenever possible, drink bottled water free of fluoridation and pollutants.

* If a cold or virus develops, you can drink freshly made vegetable juices. You and your physician may also want to try using natural herbal or homeopathic remedies. (Follow your Doctor's recommendation.)

* Individuals with candida overgrowths are probably best avoiding yeast promoting foods like sugar and other sweeteners, fluoridated water, caffeine, mushrooms, starchy and fermented foods. Understand that most commercial sauces, gravies, supplements, salad dressings, and even some spices contain added sugar and/or starch. Examples of these sugar and starch containing foods include spaghetti and taco sauces, ketchup, some dried spices and seasonings, sloppy joe mix, and meat gravies, to name a few. For more details on yeast infections read William Crook's, *The Yeast Connection*, J. Parks Trowbridge's, *The Yeast Syndrome*, and Elaine's Gottschall's, *Breaking the Vicious Cycle*.

* Fermented foods include vinegar, alcoholic beverages, sauerkraut, miso, shoyu, tofu, and sesame tahini.

* For those with chronic infections, it is probably best avoiding the mineral iron and supplement formulas which contain added iron. This is because iron supplements can potentially feed the infection.

You may instead obtain it naturally in foods like dark leafy greens, broccoli, meats, poultry, and bee pollen pellets.

* Individuals with severe or recurring illnesses frequently find it helpful to temporarily eliminate sugar and other sweeteners, alcohol, fluoridated water, as well as tobacco and caffeine products from their diets.

* Caffeine is in many products including coffee, colas, chocolate, many teas, and some soft drinks like Mountain Dew, Sunkist Orange, Dr. Pepper, as well as some painkillers. Whenever possible limit your use of these foods and products.

* Make sure that digestive enzymes are consumed daily. (Digestive enzymes are present in raw fruit, raw unfiltered honey, bee pollen, raw vegetables, sauerkraut, miso, and shoyu.) You can also obtain enzymes from digestive enzyme supplements. Check with your nutritional consultant/naturopath to determine if you would benefit from supplementation.

* Utilize a wide variety of cooking methods including steaming, sautéing, baking, broiling, grilling, boiling or poaching. Using different approaches helps to keep the body in balance.

*Arthritis sufferers may find relief by avoiding members of the nightshade family. Members of this food group include tomatoes, potatoes, peppers, except white pepper, eggplant, tobacco, and chocolate.

*Avoid black pepper, it is not digestible. This is especially important for those with gastrointestinal disturbances. Cayenne or white pepper can be used as a substitute instead.

* Reduce refined sugar and caffeine usage when possible.

* Charred foods may be carcinogenic and so are best avoided.

* All sweeteners are best consumed in moderation.

* Avoid canned foods whenever feasible; instead chose fresh and locally grown foods.

* To lessen nutritional losses, avoid thawing frozen vegetables prior to cooking.

* Iceberg lettuce is not a good source of nutrients; instead use the leaf and romaine varieties.

* People suffering with food allergies may find it helpful to keep a written journal of all items consumed. This will allow them to track their symptoms in accord with the foods eaten on particular days.

* Make your meals as colorful as possible by using a diverse range of fresh fruit and vegetables.

* Save any remaining liquid that was used to cook vegetables. It contains many of the nutrients that leached from food during cooking and so can be used as an excellent soup starter or you can just drink it.

* Iron deficiency anemia sufferers could benefit from cooking with iron pots.

* If dry roasting seeds and nuts, make only enough to last five to seven days, otherwise, they could become rancid and are not health building.

* Get a sufficient amount of sleep and rest whenever possible.

* Chew your food very well before swallowing.

* Proper maintenance of your teeth and gums is crucial to your health and well-being.

* Monitoring the condition of your digestive system, is most effectively accomplished by checking the appearance of your bowel

movements. Ideally they should be long, odorless, solid and regular. Anything different such as diarrhea, constipation, and very strong smelling odors may indicate that your digestive system is not operating at its top level. Please be aware, that initially after improving your diet, bowel odors may worsen for a period of time. This usually goes on until your body eliminates any leftover mucous or toxic bowel matter. Once the process of detoxification is completed, your movements should be as ideally described.

* Non-fiberous foods like white flour can accumulate in the gastrointestinal tract and provide an optimum environment for certain types of harmful bacteria, yeast microorganisms, worms, and parasites. All of which can contribute to unpleasant symptoms and lead to a number of health disturbances.

* Those who suffer from a severe gastrointestinal illness may initially require that their food be chewed as much as 50 times per mouthful. Failure to do this could prevent healing from taking place, in spite all of your efforts.

These are just a few of the common tips that I have found helpful to those people who are moving to a healthy way of eating. As you get more experienced with your new lifestyle you will learn many other helpful strategies for living naturally.

The Five Taste Sensations

One of the most common problems which many face is uncontrollable food cravings. Many times these compulsions make it almost impossible to stay on a healing plan. However, what we need to understand is that cravings are just another symptom of imbalance. Meaning that our body is lacking in something which it needs to return back to its proper balance. Probably the most common cause of food cravings is that the diet did not supply the body with all five taste sensations. The five taste sensations of salty, hot, bitter, sour, and sweet are our body's natural way of achieving satiation and maintaining equilibrium. Although many people achieve balance without knowledge of this principle, having a good grasp of it will make you much more efficient in attaining it.

The information below helps us achieve this task by naming the foods which contain the varying flavors. Following this chart will not only help you to balance your meals but also to make healthier decisions.

Hot - -	Horseradish, daikon, wasabi, garlic, mustard, pepper, raw onions, leeks, chives, ginger, and raw cabbage.
Sweet - -	Carrot, pumpkin, winter squash, sweet potato, fruit, and fruit juices, honey, barley malt, stevia, rice syrup, and maple syrup.
Salty - -	Sea salt, miso, tamari (shoyu), gomashio, umeboshi plums, meat, dairy, seafood, and celery.
Sour - -	Lemon, lime, and sauerkraut.
Bitter - -	Dark leafy greens.

These are some the known healthful foods which supply the five taste sensations. By learning to incorporate each of these flavors into your meals, you will usually be able to eliminate or at least control any strong cravings. This is extremely important if you want to move forward on your program, because it will give you the personal strength to adhere to your new lifestyle without deviating from its principles.

If this tool does not assist you in controlling your cravings, then other factors such as hypoglycemia, candida albicans (yeast), or nutritional deficiencies should be considered as underlying causes. To determine the basis of the problem, check with your nutritional consultant and physician.

Christopher K. Sembera (BS, CNC, Be.P)

Organizational Tips

The following is a listing of several good tips which I have found helpful to those seeking to become more efficient at managing their time.

* In the beginning, you may find it necessary to plan schedules and menus a few days in advance.

* Have domains in the kitchen set up for each food category such as a grain and bean zone, pasta and whole grain flour section, a seafood and meat area in freezer, and separate sections in refrigerator for fruits, vegetables, and greens. This will help to keep you organized for easier usage of all corresponding kitchen duties.

* Before going shopping, complete a list. Go through each food section in your house and make certain that you write everything that will be needed one day beyond the next shopping day. Then when at the store, mark everything you purchase off your list. These steps may help save you an extra trip to the store.

* Buy enough food to last at least one day beyond your next planned shopping day. This will provide you with an additional day of food, if something out of the ordinary occurs.

* Oils should be refrigerated immediately after purchase and kept no longer than four to six months. Olive oil is more stable than most other oils and does not require refrigeration.

* Dry beans and grains can be stored up to six months; freeze if you wish to keep them longer. Seeds and nuts can be stored from one to three months before freezing becomes necessary.

* Storage jars are excellent for keeping your seeds, nuts, beans, and grains dry and away from bugs.

* Complete a to-do list each night for the coming day.

* The night before your next day, review your schedule and menu; this is an effective way to prepare for the upcoming day.

* Stainless steel thermoses are excellent for preserving cooked foods when away from home.

* Buy a schedule or appointment book and carry it with you always.

* To save time, clean as you go.

* Store whole grain flours in freezer to preserve freshness.

* Fix breads and desserts on weekends or during free periods at night. Most desserts can be frozen and saved for later use.

* Make meal preparation easier by using any leftover foods in an upcoming meal. For example, after eating red beans and brown rice, you could use some of the beans to make a soup. This common sense step can help you save a tremendous amount of food and time.

* If following any type of vegetarian eating plan, always have precooked foods such as beans and grains in the refrigerator and/or freezer for unplanned changes in schedule.

LIFESTYLE SUGGESTIONS

The following lifestyle suggestions are basic tips which I have found helpful to building and maintaining good health.

* Wear all cotton clothing whenever possible. Cotton is comfortable and allows the human body to discharge toxins more effectively.

* Walk 30 minutes a day, four to six times per week. Riding a stationary bike or using a stair climber are acceptable alternatives.

* One to two times per day, rub your entire body with a cotton washcloth. This stimulates circulation and aids the skin in detoxification. If in a hurry, at least do the hands and feet.

* Those who are chemically sensitive should consider making their bedroom a chemically- free environment. There should be no carpeting in the bedroom and consider buying an air purifier with an ionizer. Use all cotton bedding, sheets, and blankets. Plus keep perfumes and/or scents out of the bedroom.

* Just because you have been told that your affliction is incurable does not necessarily mean that it cannot be healed naturally. (You may merely need to address the underlying causes of your affliction, so that your body can have an opportunity to repair itself.)

* Learn to view symptoms of discomfort as warning signals which are alerting you that your body is not functioning optimally.

* Reread and review your goals; this will help you to focus on them and maintain a positive can-do attitude.

* If your initial health plan is unsuccessful in correcting your condition, use your health team to revise your plan until you find an approach that will aid your cause.

* It will probably be necessary to make periodic adjustments in your plan as you proceed through the stages of healing.

* Bring more positive, loving, supportive people into your life by being more optimistic.

* Learn to listen to your body and address the imbalances which your body is exhibiting. Remember, this is the only body you will ever have.

* God will help you along the way; listen to your conscience for guidance.

* If chemically sensitive, avoid use of and limit exposure to harsh chemicals and household cleaners; this includes cosmetics and perfumes.

* Gas heat and appliances can cause problems for some hypersensitive people. Electric utilities and stoves are beneficial for these individuals.

* Avoid cigarette smoke and all environmental toxins whenever possible.

* If you find yourself focusing on the negative in society, go on a news fast. This can be very helpful to changing negative attitudes.

* Brush and floss your teeth regularly.

* Eliminate all toxic relationships from your life.

* In most cases, there is almost always a way to rebuild your health. It just depends upon how badly you want it and how much of an effort you are willing to expend to get it.

TIPS FOR EATING HEALTHY WHEN DINING OUT

These are just a few simple ideas that will help you make better choices when eating at restaurants.

* Avoid heavy sauces and creams; this will help you to reduce your fat intake.
* If eating a sauteed dish, request that the dish be made with olive oil as opposed to butter.
* Choose broiled, baked, and grilled meat dishes. As opposed to those which are fried.
* Eat at places that have fruit and vegetables which are not served drowning in butter.
* When eating salads, use olive oil with fresh lemon juice or vinegar as a salad dressing.

* If eating a dessert, limit yourself to a small portion.

QUESTION and ANSWER

The following is an attempt to answer the most commonly asked questions. Although it may not answer all of your concerns, it should be helpful to most of your inquiries.

Can the information in this book be used to help cure any diseases? *No. It merely supplies you with guidelines and strategies which, when used appropriately, are capable of maximizing health and assisting the healing process. This approach is not a panacea and must not be viewed as one.*

Do you recommend using natural healing methods as a substitute for traditional medical treatment? *Absolutely not! Holistic approaches are something that should only be used in addition to medical therapies. With all the benefits that each of these methods have to offer, it does not make sence to limit yourself to just one of these philosophies.*

If natural healing approaches are effective, why isn't my doctor aware of them? *Unfortunately, medical schools currently spend very little time on nutrition and prevention and instead focus heavily on drugs, surgery, and other invasive therapies. As a result, most physicians are simply not properly informed and educated about the numerous benefits of holistic approaches. This oversight thus leaves these physicians unprepared to properly educate their patients about the advantages of natural healing methods. Therefore, it is up to each of us to sufficiently learn how we can maximize our overall health and well-being.*

What type of problems could be caused by a nutritional imbalance? *It is the opinion of many of the top nutritional physicians that most chronic illnesses are in part related to severe nutritional deficiencies. Therefore, just about any recurring problem could to some extent be related to a nutritional deficiency or imbalance.*

Can you explain the concept of health imbalances and provide an example of how a health problem can actually be a sign of imbalance in the body? *This view is part of the holistic philosophy which* claims that people who are experiencing symptoms of discomfort are actually being given a warning signal that their body is not functioning optimally. If this occurs, the individual is thought to be suffering with some sort of imbalance. One such example of a health imbalance could be high blood pressure. When this is present, one thing a holistic health consultant may suspect is that the client is consuming excessive levels of sodium-rich foods but insufficient amounts of potassium-rich foods. He would then encourage the client to consume less sodium-rich foods and more potassium-rich foods. (The proper percentage for most is about 20% sodium rich foods to 80% potassium rich foods.) This is important because potassium is the opposing or balancing element to sodium. Increasing consumption of potassium would help the individual to reestablish a properly balanced level of both potassium and sodium in his body. In turn, it is hoped that this step helps to lower the client's blood pressure. This is but one example of how a natural health consultant attempts to help his client achieve balance.

How much of an effort does it take to stimulate the natural healing process? *That depends entirely upon the extent of your illness.*

Are all diseases preventable? *No. But I have come to the conclusion that the overwhelming majority of all diseases can be prevented. It is thus wise to implement these health building strategies into your life. Doing so can help reduce your risks of developing a chronic ailment. However, even if you cannot prevent a disease from occurring, you can usually improve your quality of life.*

How long does healing take? *That depends upon the overall health status and commitment of the individual but a general guideline is anywhere from 6 months to 3 years.*

Can I take breaks from my healing plan? *To help you understand this point, examine this analogy. Imagine if you had a broken leg, it was placed in a cast, and your physician told you not to walk on your injured leg for 2 months. Yet, every Sunday you removed your cast to play football. Under this scenario, how effectively would your leg heal? The answer is obviously that your leg would not heal properly, because you did not adequately adhere to your doctor's recommendation. This is precisely what happens when we stray from our wellness program. For this reason, it is* *important that we remember to stick with a productive health building routine as long as is necessary.*

Is this program a life sentence? *That largely depends upon what your goals are and what quality of life that you wish to experience. If you are ill and striving for optimum wellness then you will need to adhere to a wellness plan more stringently. However, if you have more modest goals a lesser effort is usually sufficient.*

Is there any one program that will be beneficial for everyone to follow? *Again, there is no one single healing program that works for everyone. Each individual has specific needs that must be met and therefore programs must be adjusted and individualized to meet those needs.*

Are microwave ovens safe to use? *Some health advocates insist that microwaves, especially when used for cooking, change the molecular structure of the food being prepared. If however you are going to use a microwave, you are recommended to use it only for heating of food. Those individuals who have a health problem are probably better off playing it safe and avoiding them altogether.*

You have mentioned that fluoridated water is a problem for many people and that it is not particularly helpful in terms of reducing cavities or gum disease. Then what do you suggest to help prevent dental diseases? *In addition to proper dental care such as maintaining regular dental appointments, and consistent brushing and flossing, it is also essential that a proper natural foods diet be utilized. This will help to prevent nutritional deficiencies, which is, in my opinion, at least part of the reason that dental diseases occur. Another contributor to dental problems is the presence of harmful bacteria in the mouth. It is my view that this can only be combated with diet and natural infection fighters like bovine colostrum and olive leaf extract supplements.*

Do you think that heavy metals like mercury, cadmium, aluminum, and lead should be avoided by everyone or just those with health problems? *Indeed heavy metals like aluminum, lead, cadmium, and mercury have been linked by some health advocates as possible contributors to health disturbances. Although some of these disturbances may be unsolvable, other more correctable illnesses require that* these metals be safely and effectively detoxified from our bodies in order for healing to occur. To nutritionally address this problem one must follow a well-balanced natural foods diet, with emphasis on whole unrefined foods like dark leafy greens and vegetable juices. There are also a lot of supplements which become very important for detoxifying these metals. For information on the metal eliminating elements, see your nutritional consultant and physician.

What is your opinion of the weight loss, fat absorption products? *These products concern me because fat is needed for assimilation of the fat soluble vitamins A, D, E, and K. Thus, if there is not sufficient fat to absorb these vitamins, you may be setting yourself up for deficiencies of these vitamins. If my assessment is correct, then use of these products could ultimately lead to deficiency symptoms of these nutrients. For this reason, it is my view that these products not be used.*

Why is spirituality important? *Because humans are spiritual beings who are constantly seeking to learn more about their innerselves. The only way to do this is through the process of inner growth which enhances the development of our spirituality. Once achieved, the individual will enjoy an internal peace that greatly enhances his or her life and the healing process.*

I suffer from chronic fatigue syndrome but my doctor disagrees with much of this philosophy. What should I do? *Of course, as long as you are under the care of your doctor you must follow his or her recommendations. However, if you suffer with a chronic illness and feel that you might benefit from a holistic program, then you might also consider seeking the care of a more open-minded, and hopefully more nutritionally aware, physician.*

Is there an easier way to rebuild health? *While some people, particularly those with acute ailments, will recover with the use of traditional orthodox treatments alone, many other cases instead require a combination of lifestyle modifications in conjunction with proper medical care. Which category each individual falls into merely depends upon the type of disorder as well as its level of severity.*

Implementing these strategies are very time consuming; how do you fit them into your busy schedule? *To implement these* strategies into your life, it is necessary to begin first by prioritizing your life in alignment with your values. When this is done, you will be able to see clearly what is and what is not essential to your health and happiness. This enables you to move to the next step, which is to organize your life so that you will have the required time to satisfy your top priorities. Once done, you will likely find the necessary time to satisfy all of your most important requirements.

Since the medical profession has not reached a consensus on this information, why not wait until one is reached? *I suppose that is up to you and your doctor. However, if you feel that improvements in your diet and lifestyle could help improve the quality of your life and your doctor agrees that it is harmless why not give it a two week trial?*

Where could one find a holistic physician or health practitioner, especially one with a MSA machine? *Probably the best place to help locate a competent practitioner is by contacting the Academy of Bio-Energetics. The Academy's phone number is 417-754-8469. You could also contact Bio-Meridian at 888-765-4665.*

Where do Bio-Energetic practitioners typically get their training? *Several nutritional supplement companies and some long-term practitioners offer training seminars. However, The most extensive training sessions are completed through the Academy of Bio-Energetics in Springfield, Missouri by Zenia Richler, DBE, NMD.*

If one wanted to schedule an appointment with you for a Bio-Energetic Evaluation and nutritional consultation how would they reach you? *They could contact my answering service at (504) 433-3899 and then schedule an appointment.*

CHAPTER 16
RECIPES, JUICES, AND MENUS

At this point in time, I can think of few activities that can have a more profound effect on a person's life than a conscious change in diet...Annemarie Colbin

Now that you have become acquainted with the holistic philosophy of health, it is imperative that you learn how to create nutritious, health enhancing meals. For if you do not know how to prepare whole foods in a delicious and healthful manner, then you will have great difficulty adhering to an optimum eating plan. This is obviously crucial, for without proper sustenance, you will be unable to heal, repair, grow, and funtion at your top level.

One of the quickest and most beneficial ways to nourish yourself is the consumption of fresh vegetable and fruit juices. These powerhouse drinks can provide a quick source of nutrients and enzymes which are necessary for optimum health. Although juicing does take time and money, it is well worth the investment. To evaluate this strategy, review the juicing tips and information below.

Juicing

This health strategy is one of my personal favorites, simply because it can bring dramatic results without a great deal of effort. In many cases, people who drink freshly made juices experience tremendous improvement in their health and overall well-being. For one, vegetable juices are an excellent source of nutrients, like potassium, which is extremely important to the individual who is in a weakened state. Another benefit is the tremendous increase in energy which it provides. These two reasons alone have lead many to make juicing a regular part of their lives and has become a growing phenomenon in the health and wellness industry.

Although most fruits and vegetables can be used for juicing, vegetable juices are considered to be the more effective health building juices. One reason for this is that vegetable juices contain greater quantities of minerals than do fruit juices. The other reason is because most fruit juices contain a large amount of natural sugars. Most concerned with this should be those individuals who suffer with ailments such as diabetes, hypoglycemia, chronic fatigue, or yeast problems (candida). Thus, as earlier stated, they are best taken diluted 50% with water. It should be noted though that even carrot and beet juices contain significant natural sugars and are best limited at least temporarily if diabetes, hypoglycemia, or yeast infections are present. The most commonly used vegetable and fruit juices are listed below.

Vegetables	Fruits
carrot	apple
cabbage	pineapple
celery	watermelon
beet	pear
cucumber	cantaloupe
lettuce	lemon
spinach	papaya
parsley	honeydew melon

To benefit fully from juicing several rules and procedures need to be followed. Obviously, the first step is to obtain a quality juice machine. There are numerous different brands on the market, some of the better ones include the Juiceman Juicer, the Omega, and the Champion. There are many others but these are generally recognized as the finest.

Second, it is generally best to make either just vegetable juice or fruit juice but not a combination of the two. The reason for this is because different enzymes are required for the digestion of each.

The exceptions to this rule are papaya and apple which can be mixed with vegetable juices.

Next, it is best that you juice either 30 minutes before eating or 15-30 minutes after a meal. Otherwise, it could interfere with the digestion of your meal. The fourth suggestion is to choose a variety of different vegetables, so that you will be supplying your body with a wider range of nutrients. This is helpful because you will be getting a more complete healing juice which can help to restore an even wider range of imbalances. The fifth rule recommends that you drink your juices slowly, so that they will mix thoroughly with the enzymes which are secreted by your salivary glands. This should help to increase the absorption of nutrients from the juices.

The last guideline requires that the juices be consumed immediately after juicing. Otherwise, the oxidation process will break down the enzymes and reduce the healing effects of the juice. Additionally, many juicers will leave a tremendous amount of pulp in the juice and therefore should be strained one final time. This ensures that no large pieces of vegetable pulp will be able to enter your gastrointestinal tract in an unmasticated state. The following are three of the most powerful drinks which could serve as a welcome addition to your diet.

# 1		# 2		# 3	
Carrot	10 oz	Carrot	9 oz	Carrot	8 oz
Celery	3 oz	Beet	2 oz	Celery	4 oz
Spinach	3 oz	Cucumber	5 oz	Cabbage	4 oz

At this time you may be asking why not just buy the juices premade? Because store bought juices no longer contain live enzymes. These enzymes are one of the key components which aid the healing process. Not to mention that pre-made vegetable juices are not very appealing to the taste buds. Hence, it is absolutely crucial that you buy a good juice machine and make your own fresh juices. It will make a world of difference. For additional information on juicing, see Dr. Norman Walker's, *Fresh Vegetable and Fruit Juices.*

Cooking Tips

As previously stated, it is my intention to share some helpful information on how to prepare whole natural foods. However, before preparing a meal, it is necessary that we first learn to cook some of the main ingredients of our diet, whole grains and beans.

Whole Grains

While most of the recent nutritional data supports increasing the consumption of whole grains and whole grain products, a lack of information is present on how to prepare whole foods. This oversight passively encourages people to gravitate back towards the consumption of refined grains. To solve this problem, the upcoming chart contains tips and recommendations which plainly spell out how to prepare whole grains.

Whole Grain Cooking Chart

GRAIN	WATER/GRAIN RATIO (CUPS)	COOKING TIME
Brown Rice	Two / One	50 minutes
Millet (Do not soak)	Three / One	40 minutes
Barley (Soak overnight)	Two / One	1- 1.5 hours
Whole Oats (Soak overnight)	Two / One	2 hours
Steel cut oats	Two / One	30 minutes
Rolled Oats	Two / One	15 -20 minutes
Wheatberries (Soak overnight)	Two / One	1 hour
Wild rice	Two / One	45 minutes
Couscous	One / One	1 - 10 minutes
Spelt (Soak overnight)	2.5 / One	1 hour
Rye Berries (Soak overnight)	2.5 / One	1 hour
Buckwheat	Two / One	30-40 minutes
Amaranth **(low starch)**	Two / One	30-40 minutes
Quinoa **(low starch)**	Two / One	30-40 minutes
Teff **(low starch)**	Two/ One	30 minutes

Those who are living with a prolonged illness may find it necessary to soak whole grains overnight. This will help to soften grains and remove excess starch, making them more digestible. Then before cooking, make sure that you wash, rinse, and strain grains thoroughly. Also, be sure to check for small rocks and pebbles in your grains and beans. This necessary precaution will protect your teeth from any unpleasant surprises.

Next, add grain and water together in pot, bring to a boil and add salt. The portion of salt should be 1 pinch of salt for every cup of grain. Reduce heat to low and cook for recommended time. Do not remove lid of pot while cooking, especially if using a pressure cooker. When done, remove from heat, take off lid, and allow to cool for 5-10 minutes.

* If you don't have the time to cook brown rice, you can use instant brown rice, however, it is not as nutritious as organic brown rice.

If a pressure cooker was used you must allow for pressure to fully dissipate before removing lid. Or else kaboom!

Quinoa, teff, and amaranth all have a low starch content and are better suited to those with yeast problems.

Beans

Soak beans overnight or at least 8 hours; this will again help to remove excess starch. Then pour off water and rinse until clear; do not forget to look for small rocks and pebbles. After washing and cleaning legumes, place in a pot and add three parts water to one part bean. Next, add one 8 inch strip of kombu sea vegetable to the beans. Not only will this provide the beans with far more nutrients but it will also aid in making them easier to digest. When kombu is used, it helps to prevent the gas that is commonly associated with bean consumption.

Cooking times for beans usually take about one hour for small beans like lentils, split peas, and adukis, while larger beans require about two hours. Typically, I cook my beans until the kombu completely dissolves. This way I never notice the kombu but still get all of its nutritional benefits. While most spices can be added at any time during cooking, sea salt should only be added to the beans in the last 20 minutes of cooking. Adding salt earlier than this causes the beans to become hard and difficult to digest. When seasoning beans, I usually use either garlic or bay leaf. However, feel free to experiment and use many other herbs and spices. A crock pot is also an invaluable tool for cooking beans as you can put them in pot and cook beans throughout the day. Then, six to eight hours later they are done and only need to have salt, onions, and other desired seasonings added about twenty to thirty minutes before serving.

* With the exception of string beans, legumes contain a great deal of starch and frequently need to be temporarily avoided by yeast sufferers.

* Again remember that some people will react unfavorably to a diet high in whole grains and beans and would be best suited to

some modified version of Ms. Gottschall's, *Breaking the Vicious Cycle, or* Dr. D'Amato's *Eat Right for Your Body Type.* See your nutritional consultant and physician to help determine which approach would be best for you.

Now you have instructions for the preparation of two very basic foods, beans and whole grains. The rest of this chapter is devoted to (A) incorporating whole grains into your meals, and (B) providing recipes for all of the other foods which can make up your health enhancing meals. So let's begin!

RECIPES

Because everyone has different dietary needs, there is no one healing plan that can accommodate everybody. Therefore, it is impossible to put together a number of recipes that will be helpful to each individual. For this reason, I am providing recipes which can help to maintain wellness. Those with specific dietary restrictions can use these recipes to help create meals by using only the ingredients which are within your particular healing program. Then as your health improves you can broaden your range of foods and hopefully be able to use all of the ingredients listed.

I have included in my recipes a combination of both carnivorous and vegetarian meals. As a result, each type of eater can get a small collection of examples of well-balanced nutritious eating. This should make these recipes valuable to as large a group of people as possible. However, before starting any new lifestyle enhancements, you must instead meet with your physician and nutritional consultant to develop an eating plan that will meet your needs.

Salads

Chef's Salad

1. 2 Hard boiled eggs and cheddar cheese (3-4 oz)
2. lettuce (leaf or romaine)
3. carrot slices
6. onion or green onions
7. fresh mushrooms
8. sprouts
9. tomatoes

Christopher K. Sembera (BS, CNC, Be.P)

4. cucumber slices
5. Celery slices
10. bell peppers
11. red cabbage

Serve with your favorite salad dressing.
Serves: 1

Variations:
1. Use grilled fish or chicken instead of egg and cheese.
2. Soy cheese can be used instead of cheddar cheese and served with whole grain croutons or crackers.

Side Salad

1. Spinach and/or leaf lettuce.
2. tomato.
3. sprouts.
4. cheese.
5. cucumber slices
6. mushrooms
7. celery
8. garnish with sesame or pumpkin seeds.

An excellent dish with any meal.
Serve with your favorite salad dressing.
Serves: 1

Spinach Salad

1. Spinach
2. Parmesan cheese (Optional)
3. carrots
4. fresh mushrooms

Sprinkle cheese over salad.
Serve it with your favorite salad dressing
Another excellent side dish.

SALAD DRESSINGS

Oil and Vinegar

1. olive oil
2. vinegar
3. Garnish with sesame or pumpkin seeds

Instructions: Mix equal parts vinegar with olive oil. Garnish with sesame seeds.

Variations: (1) Garlic and onions can be processed and added to mixture.

(2) Fresh lemon juice can be substituted for vinegar.

Yogurt Dressing

1. Plain yogurt (sugar and fruit free)
2. fresh squeezed lemon juice

Instructions: Mix yogurt and lemon juice. Pour over salad and serve.

SOUPS
Basic Miso Soup

1. Celery.
2. Daikon slices (Japanese radish)
3. Miso (1 tsp per person)
4. 1/4 cup of carrot slices.
5. five 1/2 cups of water.
6. garnish with chives.

Instructions: Cut vegetables into small pieces and place them into 2 quart sauce pan with water. Cook for 10-15 minutes. Pour one cup of soup into another sauce pan; the remaining four cups of soup will be saved in refrigerator for another time. Then, bring the soup in sauce pan to a light boil. Remove from flame and add miso. Allow to simmer for 2-3 minutes. Garnish with chives and serve. Serves 1.

Variation: Use different vegetables, be creative.

Chicken Noodle Soup

1. 2 mostly skinless chicken breasts.
2. 1 cup of diced celery.
3. 1/2 cup of diced onions.
4. 1/2 box of whole wheat noodles.
5. sea salt to taste.
6. 2 tsp of olive oil.
7. 1 grated carrot.
8. 2 bay leaves.
9. 2 quarts of water.
10. garnish with parsley.

Christopher K. Sembera (BS, CNC, Be.P)

Instructions: Take two chicken breasts and remove about 80% of fat and skin, leaving just a little skin and fat to add flavor. Heat oil in 4 quart sauce pan. Add onions, celery, and carrot. When onion becomes translucent add chicken breasts. Lightly brown chicken, then add water, noodles, sea salt, and bay leaves. Cook for about 1.5 hours, adding more water if necessary. When chicken is tender remove it from pot, debone and dice it. Add it back to soup and serve. Garnish with parsley. Serves 4.

Winter Squash Soup

1. 1 medium butternut squash
2. 1-2 tsps olive oil
3. 3 cups of water
4. 1/4 cup of small onions
5. 1-2 TBS shoyu
6. pinch sea salt
7. 2 bay leaves
8. garnish with parsley

Instructions: Peel and cut squash into several 2-3 inch pieces, remove seeds, and place squash with 2 cups of water in pressure cooker, cook for 20-25 minutes. If you do not own a pressure cooker, boil squash in pot for 30 minutes or until squash turns to mush with 2 cups of water. Next, heat oil in pan and add onions, cook until transparent. Then add squash and puree with potato masher, blender, or food processor. Add back to large pot, add bay leaves, pinch of salt, and more water until desired thickness is obtained, simmer for 10-15 minutes. Then add shoyu (tamari) and simmer for two more minutes.

Garnish with parsley and serve. Serves: 4

Variation: Use summer squash, and cook only for about 10 minutes in sauce pan. This will produce a lighter soup appropriate for a warm summer day.

Split Pea Soup

1. 2 cups of split peas
2. 1 tsp olive oil (optional)
3. 1 cup of sliced carrots
6. 5-6 cups of water
7. 1-2 TBS shoyu (optional)
8. several pinches of sea salt

4. ½ cup of sliced rutabaga
5. 1 TBS of sliced onions
9. 2 bay leaves (optional)
10. garnish with parsley

Instructions: After soaking split peas overnight, wash and drain them. Add 2 cups of water to split peas and cook for about 1 hour. Once beans start to breakdown add carrots, rutabagas, bay leaves, olive oil and onion, if desired. At this time, you should also add sea salt and any additional water until desired thickness is obtained. Continue cooking soup until vegetables are tender, and if you choose, add shoyu at this time. Simmer for about two more minutes and remove from fire.

Garnish with parsley and serve. Serves 4.

Tamari-Barley Soup

1. 1 cup of cooked barley
2. 4 cups of water
3. 2 TBS of tamari (shoyu)
4. ½ cup of carrot slices
5. pinch of sea salt
6. 1/4 cup of sliced onion
7. garnish with chives

Instructions: Add water to 3 quart sauce pan and bring to a boil. Then add carrot and onion slices. Cook until tender, add cooked barley and shoyu. Simmer for 2-3 minutes.

Garnish with chives and serve. Serves 2.

Variation: During winter months, 1 tsp of olive oil will make soup more warming.

Lentil Soup

1. 1 cup of lentils
2. 1 tsp olive oil (optional)
3. 2 bay leaves
4. 1/2 cup of carrots
5. 1 TBS shoyu
6. grated ginger, about 1/2 tsp
7. 2 pinches of sea salt
8. Garnish with parsley.
9. 1/4 cup of leeks or onions

Christopher K. Sembera (BS, CNC, Be.P)

Instructions: Soak beans overnight. Then wash and drain lentils. Add beans to pot with bay leaves, bring to a boil and cook for about 1 hour. Add sea salt, ginger, onion, and carrots; cook until tender. Reduce to a simmer and add shoyu. Allow 2-3 minutes for flavors to intermingle. Garnish with parsley and serve. Serves 2.

Sandwiches

Almond Butter & Jelly Sandwich

1. Almond or other nut butter. (Sugar-free)
2. Favorite fruit jelly. (Sugar-free)
3. 2 slices of whole grain bread.

Excellent protein sandwich for a hungry and physically active person.

Turkey Sandwich

1. 2 slices of whole wheat bread.
2. 3 oz. of turkey deli meat.
3. mayonnaise.
4. mustard.
5. leaf lettuce.
6. 2 tomato slices.

Instructions: Wipe mayo and mustard on both sides of bread, use as little mayo as possible. Add turkey meat, leaf lettuce, and tomatoes. Serves 1.

Turkey Burgers

1. 16 oz of ground turkey meat.
2. 4-5 whole wheat burger buns.
3. 1/2 cup of diced onions. (optional)
4. 1/3 cup of chopped bell peppers. (optional)
5. Pinch of sea salt.
6. dash of red and black pepper.
7. tomato slices.
8. mayonnaise.
9. mustard.
10. onion slices.
11. leaf lettuce.
12. pickles.

Instructions: Mix onions, turkey meat, bell peppers, and seasonings in a large mixing bowl. Then make meat mixture into 4-5 burgers. Cook burgers until no pink remains in center. Place on bun and dress burger. Goes well with baked sweet potato. Serves 2-5.

Variations: Lean ground beef, or your favorite veggie burger can replace turkey.
1 ounce of cheese can also be served on burger.

Breads

Cornbread

1. 1.5 cups of cornmeal.
2. 1/2 cup of whole wheat pastry flour
3. 4 tsps baking powder.
4. 1/2 tsp sea salt.
5. 1 cup of milk or plain yogurt.
6. 1 egg.
7. 1/4 cup of corn or safflower oil.
8. 1 TBS of barley malt or honey.

Instructions: Combine and mix all dry ingredients, then add all liquid ingredients and mix. Pour mixture into muffin tins. Bake muffins at 425 for 15-20 minutes or until golden brown. Makes about 12 muffins.

Cheesy Garlic Bread

1. 4-6 slices of whole grain bread.
2. butter
3. garlic powder (contains starch)
4. soy cheese or other cheeses
5. garnish with parsley.

Instructions: Apply butter to bread very thinly. Sprinkle garlic powder and cheese to bread slices. Place in toaster oven until cheese melts and bread turns golden brown. Remove from oven, garnish with parsley and serve. Serves 2.

Christopher K. Sembera (BS, CNC, Be.P)

Mexican Meals

Bean Chalupe's

1. 6-8 corn or whole wheat tortillas
2. 1 cup of cooked beans (lentils, kidney, pintos, black-eyes, black beans)
3. lettuce (romaine or leaf)
4. soy or other cheeses
5. tomatoes
6. green onions

Instructions: Heat beans in sauce pan, if beans are not thick, cook until mixture thickens or add kuzu, corn, or arrowroot starch. Then warm tortillas in toaster oven until crisp and golden brown. Remove tortillas from oven and dress with desired toppings. Garnish with green onions and serve. Serves 2-3.

Burrito's

1. 4 whole wheat tortillas.
2. 1/4 - 1/2 cup of water.
3. 1 cup of cooked beans. (see above list)
4. 2-4 ounces of cheese.
5. 1/8 cup of diced onion.
6. 2-3 tsp. chili powder.
7. 1 TBS of chopped cilantro.
8. 1 tsp. of cumin.
9. garnish with chives or green onion.

Instructions: Put cooked beans in pot, add cilantro, chili powder, cumin, onion and cheese. Cook for about 10 -15 minutes. Place bean mixture inside tortillas and roll into burrito shape. Heat burrito's in oven until golden brown. Remove from oven, garnish with chives and serve. Serves 2.

Taco Burgers

1. 1 lb. of ground turkey or lean beef.
2. whole wheat bread or buns.
3. sliced tomatoes.
7. 1/4 of a small onion.
8. clove of garlic.
9. chili powder.

4. leaf lettuce.
5. soy cheese or dairy cheese.
6. pinch of sea salt.
10. tsp of olive oil.
11. 1/4 tsp of cumin
12. 2-3 cups of water
13. taco sauce (Old El Paso is low in sugar)

Instructions: Heat oil in large cast iron pot. Then add chopped onions and garlic, cook until translucent. Add meat and cook until no pink remains. Next, add chili powder, cumin, sea salt, and water. Cook for about 20 more minutes so that water can dissipate and flavors can intermingle. When taco meat is done, serve on buns and add lettuce, tomatoes, cheese, and taco sauce.

Vegetarian Variation: Use package of soy tempeh instead of meat.

Whole Grain Dishes

Breakfast Cereal

1. 1-2 cups of cooked oatmeal or couscous.
2. 1/2 cup of apple juice or water.
3. 1/2 tsp of cinnamon.
4. small handful of dried fruit. (raisins, apple, or apricot)
5. garnish with chopped almonds, walnuts or pecans.

Instructions: Place cooked cereal, dried fruit, apple juice or water and cinnamon in pot and simmer for 3-5 minutes. Remove from pot, garnish with chopped almonds and serve. Serves 1-2.

Variations:
1. Instead of oats, try using cooked brown rice, barley, quinoa, millet or a mixture of two different grains.
2. Instead of apple juice use almond milk, milk, rice milk, or soy milk.

Fried Rice with Vegetables

Christopher K. Sembera (BS, CNC, Be.P)

1. 1 TBS olive or sesame oil.
2. 4 cups cooked brown rice.
3. 1/2 cup of chopped onions
4. 1 cup carrots (thinly sliced)
5. 1 clove of garlic or grated ginger
5. mushrooms. (fungi)
6. pinch of sea salt
7. shoyu (to taste)
8. garnish with parsley, and
9. sesame seeds.

Instructions: Heat oil in a cast iron or 3 quart sauce pan. Add onion, garlic or ginger, carrot, sea salt, and mushrooms to hot pan. Cook veggies until tender and transparent. Add cooked brown rice and shoyu, stir thoroughly until all ingredients are well mixed. Garnish with parsley, sesame seeds and serve. Serves 2.

Variation: Use different grains: millet, barley, couscous, or quinoa.

Fresh shrimp can also be added.

Whole Grain Salad

1. 4 cups of whole grain. (Choose one); brown rice, millet, couscous, barley, quinoa.
2. 2 cups of raw chopped veggies. (Choose 4 or 5); green onions or leeks, olives, celery, cucumber, tomato, carrot, broccoli, cauliflower, etc.
3. 1/8 - 1/4 cup of olive oil.
4. 2 umeboshi plums.
5. 1 TBS brown rice vinegar.
6. Garnish with parsley and/or sesame seeds.

Instructions: Place whole grain in large mixing bowl and add other chosen ingredients. Stir thoroughly, garnish with parsley or chives and serve.

Serves 2 - 6.

Mexican Black Beans with Millet

1. 4 cups of cooked millet.
2. 1-2 cups of cooked black beans.
3. 2 quarts of water.
4. spices: bay leaf, cumin, chili powder, garlic and sea salt to taste.

5. garnish with green onion and
6. sesame seeds.

Instructions: Place beans in pot and bring to a simmer, add herbs and mix. If beans are too thick then add water until desired thickness is obtained. When beans are done, add sea salt, then remove from pot and pour black beans in a large serving dish over millet. Garnish with green onion and sesame seeds. Serves 2-4.

Oriental Chicken

1. 1 lb. of chicken breast (cubed)
2. 6-8 cups of cooked brown rice.
3. 1/4 cup of chopped onion .
4. 1/4 cup of chopped broccoli.
5. 1/4 cup of chopped celery.
6. 1/4 cup of chopped carrots.
7. 1/4 cup of chopped mushrooms.
8. 2 TBS of sesame oil.
9. minced garlic or ginger, about 1 tsp.
10. 1 TBS of shoyu.
11. 1 cup of water.
12. garnish with sesame seeds,
13. and parsley.

Instructions: Heat oil in large cast iron pot. Then, add onion and garlic or ginger. Cook until onion is translucent, then add chicken and 1 teaspoon of shoyu. Cook until all pink in chicken has been eliminated. Next, add carrots, celery, broccoli, mushrooms and 1 cup of water. Cover pot and cook for 10-15 minutes, or until vegetables are tender. Then, remove cover and add 2 more teaspoons of shoyu. Simmer and stir for two more minutes, remove from fire and serve over brown rice. Garnish with parsley and serve.
Serves 4.

Variation: Replace chicken with shrimp.

Creole Chicken

1. 4 large skinless chicken breasts.
2. 1-2 tsps of olive oil.
3. 1/2 cup of diced onions.
4. 1/2 cup of diced celery.
5. 1/4 cup of diced bell pepper.
6. 1-2 bay leaves.
7. 1 can of stewed tomatoes.
8. 1-2 cloves of garlic.
9. sea salt to taste.
10. 1/8 tsp of cayenne.
11. 1/2 tsp of dry basil.
12. 1/2 cup of water.

Christopher K. Sembera (BS, CNC, Be.P)

Instructions: Add oil to large skillet, heat and add onions, celery, bell pepper and garlic. Cook and stir until onion is translucent. Then, add chicken breasts, cook until brown. Next, add stewed tomatoes, water, sea salt, cayenne, and basil. Cook until chicken is tender, remove and serve over brown rice or whole wheat pasta, garnish with green onions. Serves 4.

Sautéed Deep Ocean Fish

1. 6-12 ounces of fish.
2. 1-2 tsps of olive oil.
3. 1 clove of garlic.
4. 1/2 a small onion.
5. dash of red or white pepper.
6. 1 cup of white wine or water.
7. pinch of sea salt.
8. garnish with lemon wedge and parsley.

Instructions: Pour oil into frying pan. Heat pan and then add garlic, onion, sea salt, and pepper. Cook until onions become translucent, then add fish. Cook on each side until fish appears cooked, then add wine. Simmer on low for about 5-10 minutes so that flavors can intermingle. Remove from fire and garnish with lemon wedge and parsley. This goes great with brown rice. Serves 1-2.

Nori Roll

1. 1 sheet of nori (sea vegetable)
2. 1 cup of moist cooked brown rice.
3. 1/2 of chopped umeboshi plum.
4. 1/4 cup of cooked carrots. (optional)
5. 7-10 pumpkin seeds. (optional)
6. Sliced chives.

Instructions: Spread brown rice evenly over nori sheet. Next, add umeboshi plum vertically through middle of nori sheet. Also add carrots, pumpkin seeds, and chives, at this time. Roll up nori sheet into a firm roll and cut into seven pieces. Serves 1.

An excellent travel food and snack that can serve as a whole meal.

Millet with Tahini-Shoyu Sauce

1. 5 cups of cooked millet.
2. 5 TBS of sesame tahini.
3. 1 TBS of shoyu.
4. 1/3 cup of water.
5. small handful of toasted sunflower or sesame seeds. (optional)
6. garnish with parsley.

Instructions: In a measuring bowl add sesame tahini and shoyu, stir well until it makes a ball. Then add water and stir until a creamy consistency is formed. Pour over millet and if desired sprinkle sesame or sunflower seeds over top of dish. Garnish with parsley and serve. Serves 2.

Variation: Instead of millet, use whole wheat pasta or brown rice.

Cajun Shrimp Stew

1. 1 lb. of peeled shrimp or crawfish
2. 1/3 cup of olive oil.
3. 2/3 cup of unbleached white flour.
4. 2 cups of water.
5. 1/2 cup of chopped onions.
6. salt, black and red pepper to taste.
7. 2 TBS of chopped parsley.
8. 2 TBS of chopped chives.
9. 8-10 cups of cooked brown rice.

Instructions: Heat oil in large cast iron pot. Add flour and stir continuously until dark brown. Then add onions and continue stirring until onions are transparent. Now add shrimp, continuously stir shrimp until they turn pink. Add two cups of water and add seasonings, reduce heat to low and let stew simmer for 15 minutes. In a separate pot, heat cooked brown rice. Then add parsley and 1/2 of the chives to stew, allowing two more minutes for flavors to intermingle. Garnish with remaining chives and serve over brown rice. Serves 4-5.

Christopher K. Sembera (BS, CNC, Be.P)

Pasta Dishes

Vegetarian Spaghetti

1. spaghetti sauce (sugar-free)
2. 1 package of brown rice, spelt, or whole wheat pasta.
3. 4 quarts of water.
4. 1 cup of chopped fresh mushrooms.
5. 1/4 cup of chopped bell pepper.
6. garnish with chopped parsley.

Instructions: Pour entire jar of pasta sauce into 3 quart sauce pan. Add chopped mushrooms and bell peppers to sauce and bring to a low boil. Turn fire on low and allow 10 minutes for vegetables to cook.

Next, in a large pot bring water to a rapid boil. At this time, add a pinch of salt and pasta. Stir occasionally and cook to desired consistency. When it is ready, pour pasta into a colander and drain. Then in a large serving dish mix pasta with spaghetti sauce. Garnish with parsley and serve. Serves 4.

Carnivore variation: Ground turkey or beef can be added to make meat sauce.

Sautéed Pasta & Vegetables

1. 1 tsp. olive oil.
2. 1/2 cup of mushrooms.
3. 1/4 cup bean sprouts.
4. 1/2 cup of onions.
5. 2 TBS shoyu (tamari)
6. 1/2 cup of carrot sticks.
7. 4 cups of cooked whole wheat pasta
8. garnish with chives and sesame seeds.

Instructions: In a large skillet or cast iron pot, heat oil, then add onion, mushrooms, carrots, and pinch of sea salt. Cook until onions are translucent. Next, add bean sprouts and cook for about five to ten minutes. Lastly, add precooked noodles and shoyu, simmer for two more minutes and serve. Serve immediately with chives and sesame seeds for garnish. Serves 2.

Variation: Use different vegetables like broccoli, green peppers, and snow peas. Beef, shrimp, or chicken can also be sautéed.

Spelt Pasta with Tamari Broth

1. 1 bag of spelt or whole wheat pasta.
2. 1/4 cup of sliced fresh mushrooms.
3. 1 cup of chopped carrots.
4. 1/4 cup of chopped onions.
5. 1 TBS shoyu (tamari)
6. 1.25 cups of water.
7. garnish with parsley, and
8. 2 tsps of sesame seeds.

Instructions: In a saucepan add water, mushrooms, carrots and onions. Cook for about ten minutes or until veggies are tender. Then add shoyu and allow 2-3 minutes to simmer. Serve over pasta and garnish with parsley and sesame seeds. Serves 2.

Variation: Can add sautéed shrimp.

Vegetables

Boiled Vegetables

1. 1 cup of water.
2. 2 cups of your favorite vegetable combos such as (cauliflower, broccoli, and carrots), (zucchini and yellow squash), (winter squash), (green and red cabbage), (string beans and carrots), (sweet potatoes), (asparagas and carrots), etc.
3. Grated ginger. (optional)
4. pinch of sea salt.

Instructions: Bring water to a boil, once water is boiling, add vegetables of your choice, ginger, and two small pinches of salt. Cook vegetables until tender. Remove veggies from pot and serve, drink or save remaining liquid for later use as a soup stock.
Serves 2-4.

Christopher K. Sembera (BS, CNC, Be.P)

Steamed Vegetables

1. 1/2 cup of water.
2. 1-2 cups of different vegetables. (Do not steam sweet potatoes or winter squash)

Instructions: Add water, vegetables, and steamer basket to pot, bring to a boil. Cook for about 20 minutes or until vegetables are tender. Serves 2-4.

Sautéed Vegetables

1. 1-2 tsps of olive oil.
2. 1 cup of thinly sliced veggies (choose 3-4).
   (carrots, onions or leeks, bean sprouts, broccoli, snow peas, mushrooms, zucchini, string beans, cauliflower, or just greens.)
3. touch of ginger. (optional)
4. 2 tsps of shoyu. (optional)

Instructions: Heat oil in pot. Add vegetables and seasonings, cook until tender. Add shoyu and if necessary a touch of water. These vegetables can be served alone or served over grains. Serves 1-2.

Baked Sweet Potatoes

1. 2 medium to large sweet potatoes.

Instructions: Preheat oven to 350F. Wash and dry sweet potatoes. Then poke potatoes with fork multiple times so that each side has several fork holes. Next, add sweet potatoes to oven and cook for about 60 minutes or until potatoes are soft and syrup is oozing from holes. Remove from oven and allow to cool. Serves 2.

Steamed Greens

1. 2 cups of greens (kale or collards)
2. 1 cup of water.

3. garnish with sesame seeds.

Instructions: Place water in 2 quart sauce pan and bring to a boil. Slice greens and place in steamer basket. Put basket in pan with boiling water, cover lid, and cook for 1-2 minutes. Remove and serve. Serves 2.

Desserts

Those of you who wish to avoid refined sugars can simply eat fruit or stick with desserts which are sweetened with fruit and fruit juices.

Banana Pudding

1. 2 cups of almond milk, skim milk, or other milk substitutes.
2. 1/4 cup of maple syrup.
3. 2 eggs (beaten).
4. 2 TBS corn or kuzu starch.
5. 2 large ripe bananas. (sliced)
6. 1 tsp of vanilla extract.

Instructions: In a large pot add and stir milk, eggs, corn starch and maple syrup. Cook ingredients for about ten minutes or until mixture thickens. Remove pudding from heat. Add vanilla extract and allow to cool in pot. Then, add bananas and refrigerate for 3 hours, then serve. Serves 4-6.

Blueberry Couscous Cake

1. 2 cups of couscous.
2. 4 cups of apple juice.
3. 3/4 cup of water.
4. 2 cups of fresh blueberries.
5. pinch of sea salt.
6. garnish with sliced almonds.

Instructions: In a large sauce pan bring apple juice, water, and sea salt to a boil. Then, add couscous, lower flame and stir until mixture begins to thicken. Next, add blueberries and mix thoroughly. Remove from fire and pour into a glass or ceramic baking dish. Place dish in refrigerator for 1 hour, garnish with almond slices and serve. Serves 8.

Apple Bread Pudding

1. 4 cups of cubed whole wheat bread.
2. 2 cups of milk, or milk substitute.
3. 3 eggs.
4. 2 cups of peeled, cored, and cubed apples.
5. 1/2 cup of honey or maple syrup.
6. 1 TBS cinnamon.
7. 1 cup of raisins.

Instructions: Preheat oven to 350 degrees. In a large mixing bowl, add milk, honey or maple syrup, and cinnamon. In a different bowl, stir egg thoroughly. Then, add egg to large mixing bowl and stir well. Next, add bread to mixture and stir well. Allow to soak for thirty minutes. Insert apples and raisins into mixture and pour into a lightly oiled 8x12 inch baking dish. Bake for 45-50 minutes, or until top is golden brown and crisp. Serve warm or at room temperature. Serves 10-12.

Boiled & Stuffed Apples

1. 4 baking apples. (Rome, Cortlands)
2. 1.5 cups of apple juice.
3. 1/4 cup of walnuts.
4. cinnamon.
5. raisins.

Instructions: Remove core from apples, leaving peel, and place in a large sauce pan. Add apple juice, and fill apples with cinnamon, walnuts, and raisins, if desired. Cover and cook over medium heat for about 30 minutes or until apples are tender. Remove and serve. Serves 4.

Variation: Pears can be substituted for apples.

Apple Pie

Filling

1. 10 -12 baking apples.
2. 1/4 cup of water.
3. pinch of sea salt.
4. 1/2 cup of walnuts. (optional)
5. 2 TBS corn starch or kuzu.
6. 1/2 cup of honey or rice syrup.
7. 1 tsp. of cinnamon.
8. 1/2 cup of raisins.
9. 1 tsp. vanilla extract. (alcohol-free)

Crust

1. 4 cups of whole wheat pastry flour.
2. pinch of sea salt.
3. 1/4 cup of corn or safflower oil.
4. 1 cup of cold water.

Instructions: (Crust) In a large mixing bowl, add flour, sea salt, and oil. Stir until mixture is well blended, add water and mix quickly to form a ball. Knead dough for 2 minutes, then let it sit for 10 minutes before rolling out. Divide dough in half and roll one part out. Place the rolled half of dough into a well-oiled pie plate to form the bottom crust. With a fork, puncture holes into the crust so that it will cook evenly. Roll out the other half of dough as it will be used to cover the pie. It will also need to be punctured with a fork to cook evenly.

(Filling) Wash, quarter, and core apples, slice the quarters into twelfths and add to large cooking pot. Add raisins, honey or rice syrup, cinnamon, vanilla, sea salt, and walnuts; simmer for 5 minutes or until raisins swell. In a small cup add water and corn starch or kuzu, stir well and add to filling. Mix thoroughly and pour into pie crust. Add top cover of dough and puncture with a fork. Place pie in oven and bake at 350 F for 30 minutes or until top crust is golden brown. Remove pie and cool before slicing.

Blueberry Coffee Cake

Cake

1. 1 cup of whole wheat pastry flour.
2. 1 1/4 cup of unbleached white flour.
5. 1/3 cup of corn oil.
6. 1 egg.

3. 2 cups of well-drained blueberries.
4. 1/2 cup of honey or maple syrup.
9. 1/2 tsp. sea salt.
7. 1/4 cup of milk or milk substitute.
8. 2 tsp. baking powder.

Topping

1. 1/4 cup of honey or maple syrup.
2. 1/2 cup of unbleached white flour.
3. 3/4 tsp. cinnamon.
4. 2 tsp. of soft butter.

Instructions: (Cake) Mix honey or maple syrup, corn oil, and egg together. In another mixing bowl, add milk, flour, baking powder, sea salt and blueberries; mix well and combine both mixtures. Pour into a greased 9x9 inch pan.

(Topping) Mix all topping ingredients together and sprinkle over the top of cake.

Bake at 350F for approximately 45 minutes or until a toothpick can be inserted and pulled out clean.

Apple Kuzu Pudding

1. 1 large apple, cored, and diced.
2. 1 cup of apple juice.
3. 1 cup of water.
4. 1 tsp. of cinnamon.
5. 1 TBS of kuzu.

Instructions: In a 3 quart sauce pan, add apple, apple juice, water and cinnamon. Cook for 5-10 minutes or until apple is soft. Then, in a separate cup add kuzu and 1/4 cup of water, stir well and add to pudding. Stir until mixture thickens and serve. Serves 2.

Variations: Pears and nectarines can be substituted for apples.

Miscellaneous

Blueberry Pancakes

Dry Ingredients
1. 1 cup of whole wheat flour.
2. 1/3 cup of white unbleached flour.
3. 1 tsp baking powder.
4. 1 pinch of sea salt.

Wet Ingredients
5. 1 egg.
6. 1 cup of plain yogurt or milk.
7. 1/3 cup of corn oil.
8. 3/4 cup of blueberries.

Fruit Sauce

1. 1 cup of blueberries.
2. 1/4 tsp of dried ginger.
3. 1/3 cup of apple juice.
4. pinch of sea salt.
5. 1 tsp of kuzu or starch. (optional)
6. 2 tsps of maple syrup. (optional)

Instructions: In a large mixing bowl add dry ingredients and stir well. Then add wet ingredients and again stir well. If mixture is too thick, you can add more skim milk or plain yogurt. Then add mixture onto a pre-oiled hot griddle. Cook on both sides until pancakes are golden brown. Remove from flame and serve with fruit sauce.

Fruit Sauce: Place all ingredients in small sauce pan. Bring mixture to a boil and stir. Cook mixture until it thickens, about 1 minute. Yields 1 cup. Serve over pancakes.

Scrambled Eggs and Veggies

1. 2-3 eggs.
2. 1/2 a bell pepper.
3. 1 tsp of olive oil or non stick pan.
4. a few pieces of sliced onion.
5. mushrooms.
6. pinch of sea salt.

Instructions: Put oil in pan and heat. Then crack eggs, put in pot, and stir until eggs are uniformly yellow. Add sea salt, bell pepper, onion, and mushrooms. Stir mixture and cook until eggs are done. Serves 1.

Almond Milk

1. 1 cup of almonds.
2. 4 cups of water.

Instructions: Bring water to a rolling boil, add almonds and cook for five minutes. Remove almonds from water and cool. Then, peel skin off almonds and place meat of almond and remaining water in a blender. Turn on low for 30-60 seconds and strain pulp. Add more water to milk to make a full quart and refrigerate. Serves 3-4.

Almond milk goes well over cereal or just for drinking.

Hopefully, these recipes will assist you in preparing well-balanced nutritious meals that will be pleasing to your taste buds. Although these meals are quite basic there are a number of excellent whole food cookbooks on the market, which provide many more flavorful recipes. Some of my favorites are Annemarie Colbin's, *Book of Whole Meals* and Mary Estella's, *Natural Foods Cookbook*.

Menus

I have compiled a one week sample menu to show you an example of what a typical week is like for a person who follows a highly nutritious diet. This is obviously only one example as many possibilities exist for achieving well-balanced healthy meals. Nonetheless, it serves as an excellent guide for learning about a whole foods diet. If this approach is okayed by your physician, it can be used to serve as a model for planning your meals. Later, as you become more knowledgeable of nutrition, you will develop a plethora of ideas for planning and preparing a healthy spread.

H³: Health, Healing, & Happiness
The Complete Guide to Holistic Healing

	Breakfast	Lunch	Dinner	Snacks
Sunday	1. Miso soup. 2. Breakfast cereal. 3. Vegetable juice.	1. Lentils with. 2. brown rice. 3. Side salad. 4. Dried fruit.	1. Turkey burger. w/ cheese. 2. Baked sweet potato. 3. Sautéed greens. 4. Banana pudding. 5. Bancha green tea	Pecans & Fruit.
Monday	1. Breakfast cereal. 2. Vegetable juice.	1. Mexican black beans with millet. 2. Boiled veggies.	1. Cajun shrimp stew. 2. Sautéed veggies. 3. Side salad. 4. Couscous cake. 5. Bancha green tea.	Fruit.

Tuesday	1. Favorite dry cereal
	    with almond milk.
	2. Whole grain toast
	    with fruit spread.
	3. Vegetable juice.
		1. Split pea soup.
		2. Whole wheat.
		    crackers
		3. Plain yogurt.
			1. Oriental chicken.
			2. Sautéed veggies.
			3. Steamed greens.
			4. Apple Kuzu Pudding.
			5. Bancha green tea.
				Fresh
				Fruit.

Wednesday	1. Miso Soup.
	2. Whole wheat
	    bread with
	    fruit jelly.
	3. Pumpkin Seeds.
		1. Chicken noodle soup.
		2. Side salad.
		3. Baked sweet potato.
			1. Black-eyed peas.
			2. Cornbread.
			3. Whole grain salad.
			4. Steamed veggies.
			5. Apple bread pudding.
			6. Vegetable juice.
				Almonds &
				Fruit.

Thursd	1. Miso soup.
	2. Whole grain cereal
	    w/ milk.
	3. Dried fruit.
		1. Turkey sandwich
		2. Steamed veggies.
		3. Spinach salad.
		4. Bancha green tea.
			1. Creole chicken
			    with brown rice.
			2. Sautéed veggies.
			3. Steamed greens.
			4. Apple pie.
			5. Vegetable juice.
				Walnuts
				&
				Fruit.

Friday	1. Scrambled eggs
	    w/veggies.
	2. Vegetable juice.
	3. Dried fruit.
		1. Chef's salad.
		2. Cheesy garlic
		    bread.
		3. Bancha green tea.
			1. Tamari-barley soup.
			2. Spaghetti and
			    meat sauce.
			3. Sautéed veggies.
			4. Steamed greens.
			5. Blueberry coffee cake.
				Whole
				wheat
				bagel &
				Fruit

Saturd	1. Miso soup.
	2. Blueberry
	    pancakes.
	3. Fruit sauce.
		1. Beans and rice
		2. Whole wheat
		    crackers w/
		    cheese.
		3. Side salad.
		4. Vegetable juice.
			Eat out at your
			favorite restaurant.
				Fruit.

Christopher K. Sembera (BS, CNC, Be.P)

Physicians & Dentists and Holistic Practitioners

The following is a roster of some top nutritional physicians as well as companies which distribute nutritional products. Hopefully, this listing of doctors and suppliers will be able to help address whatever needs you have.

Company & Address	Products & Services	Phone number
1. American Chiropractic 3140 Garden Oaks Dr. New Orleans, LA 70131	Chiropractic Care	(504) 392-1572
2. Complementary Medical Services 3501 Severn Ave. Metairie, LA 70002	Alternative Medical Care. Chelation, EDS, Nutritional counseling, Homeopathy, Chiropractic Care, Colon Hydrotherapy, Transformational.	(504) 779-6363
3. Complementary Medical Services Mandeville, LA	Alternative Medical Care	(985) 626-1985
4. Nightingale-Conant Corp.	Inspirational books and tapes.	1-800-525-9000
5. Rogers, Sherry A., M.D. 2800 W. Genesee St. Syracuse, New York 13219	Environmental Medicine (Available for phone consultations)	(315) 488-2856
6. Arthur Scott, DDS. 3939 Houma Blvd. Metairie, LA 70006	Mercury-free dental work, IAOMT member	(504) 888-1414

Recommended Reading

Aihara, Herman. *Basic Macrobiotics.* Japan Publications, Inc. 1985.

Airola, Paavo. *Every Woman's Book.* Health Plus Publishers. 1979.

Airola, Paavo. *How To Get Well.* Health Plus Publishers. 1974.

Bailey, Covert. *Smart Exercise.* Houghton Mifflin Co. 1994.

Bland, Jeffrey Ph.D., *Your Health Under Seige.* The Stephen Greene Press. 1980.

Borysenko, Joan Ph.D., *Minding the Body, Mending the Mind.* Addison Wesley Publishers. 1987.

Brandon, Nathaniel Ph.D., *Honoring The Self.* Bantam Books. 1985.

Clark, Daniel G., M.D., and Kaye Wyatt. *Colostrum Life's First Food.* CNR Publishing. 1996.

Clife, Albert E., *Let Go and Let God.* Simon & Schuster. 1979.

Colbin, Annemarie., *The Book of Whole Meals.* Ballantine Books. 1979.

Colbin, Annemarie., *Food and Healing.* Ballantine Books. 1986.

Crook, William G., M.D., *The Yeast Connection.* Vintage Books. 1983.

Davis, Adelle., *Let's Eat Right To Keep Fit.* Signet. 1970.

Davis, Adelle., *Let's Get Well.* Signet. 1972.

Diamond, Harvey & Marilyn., *Fit For Life.* Warner Books. 1985.

Dyer, Wayne Dr., *The Sky's The Limit.* Pocket Books. 1981.

Eadie, Betty J., *Embraced By The Light.* Gold Leaf Press. 1992.

Christopher K. Sembera (BS, CNC, Be.P)

Freeman, Eileen Elias., *Touched By Angels*. Warner Books. 1993.

Girzone, Joseph F., *Never Alone*. Doubleday. 1994.

Gottschall, Elaine B.A. M.Sc. *Breaking The Vicious Cycle*. Kirkton Press. 1994.

Haas, Robert Dr., *Eat To Win*. Signet. 1985.

Heimlich, Jane., *What Your Doctor Won't Tell You*. Harper Collins. 1990.

Hubbard, Ruth and Wald, Elijah., *Exploding The Gene Myth*. Beacon Press. 1993.

Jensen, Bernard D.C., Nutritionist, *Tissue Cleasing Through Bowel Management*. Bernard Jensen Enterprises. 1981.

Kushi, Michio., *The Macrobiotic Way*. Avery Publishing Group. 1985.

Lakein, Alan., *How To Get Control Of Your Time and Your Life*. Penguin Books. 1993.

McGinnis, Alan Loy., *The Power of Optimism*. Harper Collins. 1990.

Null, Gary., *No More Allergies*. Villard Books. 1992.

Ornish, Dean M.D., *Eat More, Weigh Less*. Harper Collins Publishers. 1993.

Peale, Norman Vincent., *The Power of Positive Thinking*. Fawcett Crest Books. 1963.

Powter, Susan., *The Pocket Powter*. Simon & Schuster. 1994.

Rogers, Sherry A., M.D., *The E.I. Syndrome*. Prestige Publishers. 1986.

Rogers, Sherry A., M.D., *Tired or Toxic*. Prestige Publishers. 1990.

Rogers, Sherry A., M.D., and Gallinger, Shirley., *Macro Mellow*. Prestige Publishers. 1992.

Rogers, Sherry A., M.D., *Wellness Against All Odds*. Prestige Publishers. 1994.

Seigel, Bernie M.D., *Love, Medicine & Miracles*. Harper & Row. 1989.

Smith, Kathy with Susanna Levin., *Walkfit For A Better Body*. Warner Books. 1994.

Trowbridge, John P., M.D., and Walker, Morton., D.P.M., *The Yeast Syndrome*. Bantam Books. 1986.

Wade, Carlson., *Health From The Hive*. Keats Publishing Co. 1992.

Walker, N.W., D.Sc., *Fresh Vegetable and Fruit Juices*. Norwalk Press 1978.

Young-Sowers, Meredith L., *Spiritual Crisis*. Stillpoint. 1993.

Christopher K. Sembera (BS, CNC, Be.P)

Bibliography

Adams, Ruth., *Drink To Your Health.* Better Nutrition for Today's Living. March 1993.

Adams, Ruth., *Going Organic.* Better Nutrition for Today's Living. May 1993.

Adams, Ruth., *Whole Grain Cereals, Packed With Nutrients.* Better Nutrition for Today's Living. January 1994.

Adams, Ruth., *Whole Grains, essential & delicious.* Better Nutrition for Today's Living. November 1993.

Aesoph, Lauri M., N.D., *Antioxidants, Diet & Cancer.* Delicious. July/August 1993.

Aesoph, Lauri M., N.D., *Can Dietary Fat Cause Illness?* Delicious. July/August 1993.

Aesoph, Lauri M., N.D., *Guess Who's Coming To Dinner?* Delicious. April 1993.

Aihara, Herman. *Acid and Alkaline.* George Oshawa Macrobiotics Foundation. 1971.

Aihara, Herman. *Basic Macrobiotics.* Japan Publications, Inc. 1985.

Airola, Paavo., *Every Woman's Book.* Health Plus Publishers. 1979.

Airola, Paavo., *How To Get Well.* Health Plus Publishers. 1974.

Anderson, Joan Wester., *Where Angels Walk.* Ballantine Books. 1992.

Anthony, Robert Dr., *The Ultimate Secrets of Total Self-Confidence.* Berkley Books. 1984.

Christopher K. Sembera (BS, CNC, Be.P)

Anti-Oxidants Provide Many Health Benefits. Better Nutrition for Today's Living. February 1993.

Arnold, Kathryn., *Family Meal Makeover.* Delicious. September 1994.

Arnold, Kathryn., *The Mediterranean Diet and Your Heart.* Delicious. February 1995.

Arnold, Kathryn., *What Your Doctor Never Told You About Breast Cancer.* Delicious. October 1994.

Bailey, Covert., *Smart Exercise.* Houghton Mifflin Co. 1994.

Balch, James F., M.D., and Balch, Phyllis A., C.N.C., *Prescription For Nutritional Healing.* Avery Publishing. 1990.

Barkie, Karen E., *Sweet and Sugar-free.* St. Martin's Press. 1982.

Barnard, Neal., M.D., *Eat All You Want and Lose Weight.* Natural Health. 1993.

Baylor, Curtis., M.D., *Common Sense Medicine.* Simon & Schuster. 1969.

Benedict, Dirk., *Confessions of a Kamikaze Cowboy.* Avery. 1991.

Benis, Warren. *On Becoming A Leader.* Addison-Wesley Publishing Company, Inc. 1989.

Beta Carotene Is Strong Adversary Of Cancer. Better Nutrition for Today's Living. March 1993.

Bittman, Mark., *To Your Health.* Natural Health. May/June 1992.

Bland, Jeffery, Ph.D., *Do Empty Calories=Empty Headed Kids?* Delicious. September 1991.

Bland, Jeffery, Ph.D., *Solve Digestive Problems With Probiotics.* Delicious. October 1995.

Bland, Jeffrey., Ph.D., *The Mystery of Chronic Fatigue Syndrome.* Delicious. March 1994.

Bland Jeffery, Ph.D., *What's All The Fuss About Hydrogenated Oils?* Delicious.
January/February 1993.

Bland, Jeffery, Ph.D., *Your Health Under Seige.* The Stephen Greene Press. 1980.

Borysenko, Joan Ph.D., *Minding the Body, Mending the Mind.* Addison Wesley Publishing Comp. 1987.

Braly, James., M.D., *Can Depression Make You Sick.* Delicious. March 1993.

Brandon, Nathiel Ph.D., *Honoring The Self.* Bantam Books. 1985.

Breast Cancer May Be a Preventable Disease. Better Nutrition for Today's Living. November 1992.

Bucco, Gloria., *Can You Heal Your Heart?* Delicious. January/February 1992.

Bucco, Gloria., *The Margarine Myth.* Delicious. Jan/Feb 1993.

Bucco, Gloria., *Invest In The Earth.* Delicious. April 1992.

Buscaglia, Leo. *Love.* Fawcett Crest Books. 1972.

By the editors of Consumer Guide., *Prescription Drugs.* Consumer Guide Health Series. 1991.

Challem, Jack., *Cure Carpal Tunnel Syndrome.* Natural Health. July/August 1993.

Challem, Jack and Lewin, Renate., *What's Missing from RDAs?* Jan/Feb 1993.

Cheraskin, E., M.D., Ringsdorf, W.M., D.M.D. with Arline Brecher. *Psychodietics*. Bantam Books. 1974.

Cheraskin, E., M.D., Ringsdorf, W. M., D.M.D., Clark, J.W., D.D.S., *Diet and Disease*. Keats Publishing Inc. 1968.

Chopra, Deepak M.D., *Magical Mind, Magical Body*. Nightingale-Conant Audiotape Series. 1990.

Clark, Daniel G., M.D., and Kaye Wyatt, *Colostrum Life's First Food*. CNR Publishing. 1996.

Cliffe, Albert E., *Let Go and Let God*. Simon & Schuster. 1979.

Colbin, Annemarie. *The Book of Whole Meals*. Ballantine Books. 1979.

Colbin, Annemarie. *Food and Healing*. Ballantine Books. 1986.

Cole, Beverly., *Eating For Energy*. Delicious. March 1994.

Connaly, David. *In Search Of Angels*. Perigee Books. 1993.

Crook, William G., M.D., *The Yeast Connection*. Vintage Books. 1983.

Crook, William G., M.D., Jones, Marjorie H., R.N., *The Yeast Connection Cookbook*. Professional Books. 1989.

Davis, Adelle. *Let's Eat Right To Keep Fit*. Signet. 1970.

Davis, Adelle. *Let's Get Well*. Signet. 1972.

Davis, Adelle. *Let's Have Healthy Children*. Signet. 1951.

DeAngelis, Barbara Ph.D., *Are You The One For Me?* Island Books. 1992.

Diamond, Harvey & Marilyn., *Fit For Life.* Warner Books. 1985.

Diamond, John M.D., *Your Body Doesn't Lie.* Warner Books. 1979.

Dietary Fat May Be Linked To Breast Cancer. Natural Health. March/April 1994.

Doctors Fail Nutrition. Natural Health. September/October 1993.

Dossey, Larry M.D., *The Science of Prayer.* Natural Health. March/April 1994.

Dreher, Henry., *Why Did the People Of Rosetta Live So Long.* Natural Health. March/April 1993.

Dufty, William., *Sugar Blues.* Warner Books. 1975.

Dyer, Wayne Dr., *The Sky's The Limit.* Pocket Books. 1981.

Eadie, Betty J., *Embraced By The Light.* Gold Leaf Press. 1992.

Estella, Mary., *Natural Foods Cookbook.* Japan Publications. 1978.

Finn, Kathleen., *Antibiotics: Too Much Of A Good Thing?* Delicious. 1995.

Finn, Kathleen., *Journey to Wellness.* Delicious. September 1995.

Fitzgerald, Frances., *Exercise: Your mental health epends upon it.* Health Counselor. Vol. 7, No. 5.

FitzGerald, Frances., *Healthy Digestion.* Health Counselor. Vol. 4, No. 6

Fredericks, Carlton Ph.D., *Psycho-Nutrition.* Grosset & Dunlap. 1976.

Christopher K. Sembera (BS, CNC, Be.P)

Fredericks, Carlton Ph.D., *Nutrition Guide For The Prevention & Cure Of Common Ailments & Diseases.* Simon & Schuster. 1982.

Freeman, Eileen Elias., *Touched By Angels.* Warner Books. 1993.

Fruits and Vegetables Fight Some Cancers. Better Nutrition for Today's Living. October 1993.

Gazella, Karolyn., *Brain Power.* Health Counselor. Vol. 7, No. 5.

Gazella, Karolyn A., *Controlling Candida Naturally.* Health Counselor. Vol. 7, No. 3

Girzone, Joseph F., *Never Alone.* Doubleday. 1994.

Gittleman, Ann Louise., M.S., C.N.S., *This healthcare expert wants you to ADD fat to your diet.* Health Counselor. Vol. 7, No. 3

Goldsmith, Joel S., *Living Between Two Worlds.* Harper & Row Publishers. 1974.

Golos, Natalie & Golbitz, Frances Golos., *If This Is Tuesday It Must Be Chicken.* Keats Publishing, Inc. 1983.

Gottschall, Elaine B.A., M.Sc. *Breaking The Vicious Cycle.* The Kirkton Press. 1994.

Graham, Billy. *Angels, God's Secret Agents.* Word Publishing. 1986.

Graham, Helen., *Discover Your True Needs Through Imagery.* Natural Health. July/August 1993.

Gregory, Scott J., O.M.D., *A Holistic Protocol for The Immune System.* Tree of Life Publications. 1989.

Haas, Robert Dr. *Eat To Win.* Signet. 1985.

Hausmann, Patricia M.S., *The Right Dose, How To Take Vitamins & Minerals Safely*. Ballantine Books. 1987.

Heimlich, Jane., *What Your Doctor Won't Tell You*. Harper Collins. 1990.

Hill, Napoleon & Stone, W. Clement., *Success Through A Positive Mental Attitude*. Nightingale-Conant Audiotapes.

Hill, Napoleon., *The Science Of Personal Achievement*. Nightingale-Conant Audiotapes.

Hoffer, Abram Ph.D., M.D., and Walker, Morton D.P.M., *Orthomolecular Nutrition*. Keats Publishing Inc. 1978.

Hoffer, Abram., M.D., Ph.D., *The Megavitamin Revolution*. Health Counselor. Vol. 5, No. 3.

Howell, Edward Dr., *Enzyme Nutrition*. Avery. 1985.

Hubbard, Ruth and Wald, Elijah., *Exploding The Gene Myth*. Beacon Press. 1993.

Hydrogenated Oils May Promote Heart Disease. Better Nutrition for Today's Living. July 1993.

Is Fluoridation Really Anglo-Saxon Madness? Better Nutrition For Today's Living. July 1993.

Jensen, Bernard D.C., *Arthritis, Rheumatism and Osteoporosis*. Bernard Jensen Enterprises. 1986.

Jensen, Bernard D.C., *Doctor-Patient Handbook*. Bernard Jensen Enterprises. 1984.

Jensen, Bernard D.C., and Anderson, Mark. *Empty Harvest*. Avery Publishing Group. 1990.

Jensen, Bernard D.C., *Love, Sex & Nutrition*. Bernard Jensen Enterprises. 1988.

Jensen, Bernard D.C., *Tissue Cleasing Through Bowel Management*. Bernard Jensen, Enterprises. 1981.

Kissir, Susan., *Treat Alcoholism With Nutrition*. Natural Health. Jan/Feb 1993.

Kline, Morton A., *Vitamin Phobia*. Natural Health. January/February 1994.

Knaster, Mirka., *Food To Improve Your Mood*. Natural Health. Sept/Oct 1993.

Krieger, Delores Ph.D., R.N., *The Therapeutic Touch*. Prentiss Hall Inc., 1979.

Kushi, Aveline and Esko, Wendy. *The Changing Seasons, Macrobiotic Cookbook*. Avery. 1985.

Kushi, Michio., *How To See Your Health, Book of Oriental Diagnosis*. Japan Publications. 1980.

Kushi, Michio., *Natural Healing Through Macrobiotics*. Japan Publications. 1978.

Kushi, Michio., *The Macrobiotic Way*. Avery Publishing Group. 1985.

Kushi, Michio., *Your Face Never Lies*. Avery Publishing Group. 1983.

Lakein, Alan., *How To Get Control Of Your Time and Your Life*. Penguin Books. 1993.

LeShan, Lawrence., *How To Meditate*. Bantam Books. 1974.

Leshowitz, Eric., M.D., *The Power of Touch*. Natural Health. March/April 1994.

Lieberman, Shari & Bruning, Nancy., *The Real Vitamin & Mineral Book*. Avery. 1990.

Maltz, Maxwell M.D., *Psychocybernetics*. Pocket Books. 1969.

Many Researchers Urge That RDAs Be Elevated. Better Nutrition for Today's Living. January 1994.

Marr, Liz R.D., M.S., *10 Questions About Fats & Oils*. Delicious. August 1994.

Marshall, Catherine., *A Closer Walk, A Spiritual Lifeline To God*. Avon Books. 1986.

McCaleb, Rob., *ECHINACEA popular, potent herbal extract*. Better Nutrition for Today's Living. January 1994.

McCaleb, Rob., *GOLDENSEAL medicinal herb*. Better Nutrition for Today's Living. November 1993.

McCaleb, Rob., *Herbs To Keep You Healthy*. Delicious. August 1995.

McCaleb, Rob., *The World's Tastiest Medicine*. Delicious. February 1995.

McCaleb, Rob., *Two Immune-Enhancing Herbs*. Delicious. December 1995.

McCaleb, Rob., *Upset Stomach? Try Ginger*. Delicious. June 1995.

McDougall, John A., M.D., *The McDougall Program*. Penguin Books. 1990.

McGinnis, Alan Loy. *The Power of Optimism*. Harper Collins. 1990.

Mindell, Earl., Ph.D., *Earl Mindell's, Quick and Easy Guide to Better Health*. Keats Publishing. 1978.

Mindell, Earl., Ph.D., *Earl Mindell's, Vitamin Bible*. Warner Books. 1991.

Mindell, Earl., R.Ph., Ph.D., *Herbal Teas*. New Hope Communications. October 1992.

Minerals are Esssential for our Optimum Health. Better Nutrition For Today's Living. November 1992.

Moyers, Bill., *Healing and The Mind*. Doubleday. 1993.

Murray, Frank., *Antioxidants Provide Many Health Benefits.* Better Nutrition for Today's Living. February 1993.

Murray, Frank., *Minerals Are Essential For Our Optimum Health.* November 1992.

Murray, Michael T., N.D., *Healing Ulcers Naturally.* Health Counselor, Vol. 4, No. 6.

Nelson, Katherine., *Coping with Food Allergies and Sensitivities.* Delicious. April 1994.

Never underestimate the power of garlic. Health Counselor. Vol. 5, No. 2.

Nightingale, Earl., *The Strangest Secret for Succeeding in the World Today*. Nightingale-Conant Audiotapes.

Null, Gary. *No More Allergies*. Villard Books. 1992.

Null, Gary and Steven. *How To Get Rid Of The Poisons In Your Body.* Simon and Schuster. 1977.

Nussbaum, Elaine., *Recovery From Cancer.* Avery Publishing. 1992.

Nutritional Therapy Shows Promise For CFS. Better Living for Today's Living. Feb 1993.

Organic Foods Have More Minerals. Natural Health. Sept/Oct 1993.

Ornish, Dean M.D., *Eat More, Weigh Less.* Harper Collins Publishers. 1993.

Oski, Frank A., M.D., *Don't Drink Your Milk.* Teach Services. 1983.

Otto, James H. & Towle, Albert. *Modern Biology.* Holt, Rinehart, and Winston Publishers. 1973.

Patterson, Eric., *The Pesticide & Breast Cancer Equation.* Delicious. October 1994.

Pauling, Linus. *Vitamin C and the Common Cold.* Berkely Publishing Corp. 1970.

Pauling, Linus. *How To Live Longer and Feel Better.* Avon Books. 1987.

Peale, Norman Vincent. *The Power Of Positive Thinking.* Fawcett Crest Books. 1963.

Pesticide Residues Are Linked to Breast Cancer. Better Nutrition For Today's Living. November 1993.

Pfeiffer, Carl C., M.D., *Nutrition and Mental Illness.* Healing Arts Press. 1987.

Pike, Arnold Dr., *Controlling Yeast Infections.* Let's Live. May 1991.

Pizzaro, Lara., M.A. *Power Up Your Immune System.* Delicious. October 1995.

Powter, Susan. *The Pocket Powter.* Simon & Schuster. 1994.

Christopher K. Sembera (BS, CNC, Be.P)

Produce Without Problems Going Organic. Better Nutrition for Today's Living. May 1993.

Quillin, Patrick., Ph.D., R.D., *The Role of Nutrition in Cancer Treatment.* Health Counselor. Vol. 4, No. 6

Rapp, Doris., M.D., *Is This Your Child.* William Morrow and Company Inc. 1991.

Rea, William., M.D., and Golos, Natalie., *Success In The Clean Bedroom.* Pinnacle Publishers. 1992.

Richmond-Coca, Blanca R.D., *Eat More & Lose Weight.* Delicious. October 1992.

Robbins, Anthony., *Unlimited Power.* Nightingale-Conant Audiotapes.

Roman, Sanaya., *Spiritual Growth.* H.J. Kramer. Inc., 1989.

Rogers, Jacquelyn., *You Can Stop Smoking.* Pocket Books. 1987.

Rogers, Sherry A., M.D., *The E.I. Syndrome.* Prestige Publishers. 1986.

Rogers, Sherry A., M.D., *The Cure Is In The Kitchen.* Prestige Publishers. 1991.

Rogers, Sherry A., M.D., *You Are What You Ate.* Prestige Publishers. 1988.

Rogers, Sherry A., M.D., *Tired or Toxic.* Prestige Publishers. 1990.

Rogers, Sherry A., M.D., and Gallinger, Shirley., *Macro Mellow.* Prestige Publishers. 1992.

Rogers, Sherry A., M.D., *Wellness Against All Odds.* Prestige Publishers. 1994.

Rusk, Tom., M.D., *A Coach For the Human Spirit.* Natural Health. July/August 1993.

Rusk, Tom M.D., with D. Patrick Miller. *The Power of Ethical Persuasion.* Penguin Books. 1993.

Sachs, Judith. *What Women Should Know About Menopause.* Dell Publishing. 1991.

Sattilaro, Anthony J., M.D., with Tom Monte, *Recalled By Life.* Avon Books. 1982.

Schecter, Steven., *Is Your Water Supply Contaminated?* Natural Health. Nov/Dec 1993.

Scheer, James F., *Bee Pollen, health from the hive.* Better Nutrition for Today's Living. May 1993.

Scheer, James F., *Bee Propolis, praised healing agent.* Better Nutrition for Today's Living. September 1993.

Scheer, James., *our second immune system ACIDOLPHILUS.* Better Nutrition for Today's Living. November 1992.

Scheer, James F., *Royal Jelly, health and life enhancer.* Better Nutrition for Today's Living. December 1993.

Schuller, Robert H., *Life's Not Fair, But God Is Good.* Bantam Books. 1991.

Schuller, Robert H., *Tough Times Never Last But Tough People Do!* Bantam Books. 1983.

Seamens, Dan., *Do You Need to Supplement Your Diet?* Natural Health. Nov/Dec 1993.

Seamens, Dan., *Eating For Optimum Health.* Natural Health. Nov/Dec 1992.

Seigel, Bernie M.D., *Love, Medicine & Miracles*. Harper & Row. 1986.

Seigel, Bernie M.D., *Peace, Love & Healing*. Harper And Row. 1989.

Smith, Kathy with Susanna Levin. *Walkfit For A Better Body*. Warner Books. 1994.

Smith, Lendon M.D., *Feed Your Kids Right*. Dell Publishing. 1979.

Spalding, Levona., *How Eating Right Improved My Arthritis*. Delicious. Nov 1994.

Steinman, David., *Organic Foods Have More Minerals*. Natural Health. Sept/Oct. 1993.

Taylor, Terry Lynn., *Answers From The Angels*. H.J. Kramer Inc., 1993.

Tenney, Louise., M.H., *Today's Herbal Health*, Woodland Books. 1992.

The Columbia University College of Physicians and Surgeons. *Complete Home Medical Guide*. Crown Publishers. 1985.

The New American Bible. Thomas Nelson Publishers. 1983.

Thomson, Bill., *Debating Evening Primrose Oil*. Natural Health. Nov/Dec 1992.

Thomson, Bill., *How Antioxidants Fight Disease*. Natural Health. Sept/Oct 1992.

Thomson, Bill., *Rejuvenate Yourself in Three Weeks*. Natural Health. Jan/Feb 1993.

Thompson, William., *A New Farm Philosophy*. Delicious. October 1992.

Tieger, Paul D. & Barron-Tieger, Barbara., *Do What You Are.* Little, Brown and Company. 1992.

Trace Analysis. Natural Health. September/October 1993.

Tracy, Brian., *How to Master Your Time.* Nightingale-Conant Audiotapes.

Tracy, Brian., *The Science of Self-Confidence.* Nightingale-Conant Audiotapes.

Trowbridge, John P., M.D., and Walker, Morton., D.P.M., *The Yeast Syndrome.* Bantam Books. 1986.

Vukovic, Laurel., *Aging Gracefully.* Natural Health. July/Aug 1993.

Vukovic, Laurel., *Maintain a Healthy Gut.* Natural Health. May/June 1993.

Wade, Carlson., *Bee Pollen and Your Health.* Keats Publishing Inc. 1978.

Wade, Carlson., *Health From The Hive.* Keats Publishing Inc. 1992.

Waitley, Denis Dr., *The Psychology Of Winning.* Berkley Books. 1984.

Walker, N.W., D. Sc. *Fresh Vegetable and Fruit Juices.* Norwalk Press. 1978.

Ward, Bernard., *Think Yourself Well, The Amazing Power Of Your Mind.* Globe Communications Corp. 1994.

Waring, Nancy., *The Warrior Who Conquered Stress.* Natural Health. Sept/Oct 1992.

Water Fluoridation is a Potential Threat. Better Nutrition for Today's Living. March 1992.

Christopher K. Sembera (BS, CNC, Be.P)

Webster's Collegiate Dictionary. G. & C. Merriam Co., Publishers. 1953.

Wegscheider-Cruce, Sharon. *Learning To Love Yourself.* Health Communications, Inc. 1987.

Wood, Rebecca., *Eating Well Despite Food Allergies.* Sept/Oct 1992.

Yogurt Cure for Candida. Natural Health. July/August 1992.

Young-Sowers, Meredith L., *Spiritual Crisis.* Stillpoint. 1993.

ABOUT THE AUTHOR

The author, earned a BS. degree in Education from Our Lady of Holy Cross College in 1989. He also completed nutritional health programs from the American Holistic College of Nutrition in 1993 and is a Certified Professional member of the American Association of Nutritional Consultants. He has completed his Bio-Energetic Practitioner certification through the Academy of Bio-Energetics in Springfield, Missouri. Mr. Sembera is the owner of Natural Health Consulting. He presently performs Bio-Energetic health testing and nutritional consultations for his clients in three health facilities. Complementary Medical Services in Metairie, and Mandeville, Louisiana and the American Chiropractic Clinic in New Orleans. To schedule an appointment for a Bio-Energetic Evaluation call (504) 433-3899.